"Storytelling is at the essence of our human experience and of connecting us one to another. Powerful stories, told with true authenticity enrich lives and strengthen communities. Vision Loss Resources' book is filled with inspiring stories that are a gift to all of us. Reading it you will come away with a wealth of perspectives and truths in the lives of those living with vision loss. As our population ages, we all will benefit from greater empathy and understanding as vision loss affects even more people across our communities."

— **LUCY SWIFT**, vice president of Minnesota Productions and Partnerships, Minnesota Public Television

"*The Way We See It* is an honest, candid look at vision loss from the perspective of individuals who live with it every day. You will be inspired by their stories, their insights, and their determination. This thoughtful compilation of stories captures the resiliency of the human spirit and the value of community support."

— **MARLA RUNYAN**, author of *No Finish Line*, two-time U.S. Olympian, legally blind since age nine

D1085809

The Way We See It

The Way We See It

A Fresh Look at Vision Loss

Book production manager: Andrea Rud
Copy editor: Sally Heuer
Designer and typesetter: Judy Gilats
Editors: Wendy Brown-Báez, Pamela Fletcher,
and Patricia Kirkpatrick
Publisher: Kimberly Nightingale

ISBN 978-0-9888681-1-3 (print)
ISBN 978-0-9888681-5-1 (audio)
ISBN 978-0-9888681-6-8 (e-book)

Printed in the United States of America

Arcata Press | Saint Paul Almanac
275 East Fourth St., Suite 701
Saint Paul, MN 55101
www.arcatapress.org

Saint Paul Almanac is a subsidiary of Arcata Press,
a nonprofit publisher.

DEDICATION

These stories reveal the heart and soul
of all the people we have served at Vision
Loss Resources. This book is dedicated
to the clients, staff, founders, and benefactors
who have supported the mission, the people
and the progress of Vision Loss Resources
for 100 years.

— Kate Grathwol, PhD, President/CEO,
    Vision Loss Resources

CONTENTS

PREFACE

How This Book Began

Sometimes when you plant a lone seed, there is no way of knowing what may sprout. Imagination was the seed, and conversation the catalyst, when four companions/volunteers at Vision Loss Resources exclaimed, "We have so many stories to tell, we could write a book!"

After numerous discussions regarding our significant life changes, tales of loss and ultimate acceptance, embarrassing moments, and (save the best for last) truly funny incidents, we realized that it would clearly be cathartic and fun for us to put all of these stories into a book. Moreover, it could be very helpful to share our thoughts with the interested public, especially those who have been impacted by visual impairment or total blindness. That was the charm—that it would be good for other people, as well as for us. The decision was made. "We *will* write a book."

We had the inspiration, but next we needed collaboration and dedication, so we began by forming a committee of seven volunteers. We engaged the staff, and then reached out to others in the community to join us in writing a collection of real-life stories.

The authors of this anthology are a mix of not only the blind and visually impaired, but also family members, friends, and coworkers—the people who know us best. As the saying goes, "Everyone's got a story."

We hope this book will inform, inspire, and entertain you, and leave you with a fresh new look at vision loss as seen through our eyes.

Vision Loss Resources History

Vision Loss Resources sprang from the 1992 merger of the Saint Paul Society for the Blind and the Minneapolis Society for the Blind, organizations that enjoyed broad support from individuals and community groups. Two people were pivotal figures in founding the Minneapolis society—Helen Keller and Thomas Schall, later United States Senator Schall.

According to *The First Sixty Years: The Minneapolis Society for the Blind*, lawyer Schall—blinded by an accident with electricity—approached Mrs. A. W. (Grace Swift) Strong and Fred Nash of the Nash-Finch Company in 1913, with the intent "to interest them in developing a volunteer group to work with and for the blind citizens of Minneapolis."

But it was Helen Keller's visit to Minneapolis in 1914 that many credit with inspiring the establishment of the Minneapolis society. The Woman's Club of Minneapolis brought Keller to speak at the Shubert Theater in January 1914. Keller's visit, a newspaper reported on January 11, "has added impetus to the work of the organization for the blind and much is being planned for the society within the next few months."

The Saint Paul Society for the Blind (SPSB) seems to have been a successor of Mutual Aid Blind Association (MABA), founded about 1918. A newspaper noted "the association . . . will endeavor to promote education and training for the blind and near blind by means of training centers and will co-operate with the state and the state department of re-education."

The association received early support from the Council of Jewish Women. Peggy Larson, who compiled information on the SPSB, credited Esther Frankel, associated with the Council of Jewish Women, as being "instrumental in locating . . . individuals in need of service." For a fundraiser for the MABA at the Masonic Temple at Sixth and Smith Avenues, a long list of women "well known in social, philanthropic and club circles will be patronesses for the event." As a newspaper noted, the "association is a co-operative organization representing clubs and charities that has accomplished much for the city's blind residents."

The Woman's Club has been involved with present-day Vision Loss Resources from its founding as the Minneapolis Society for the Blind. The club put its considerable resources and support behind the society, as did other women's groups in the Twin Cities. On March 14, 1914, the Woman's Club gave its first annual luncheon for visually impaired people, a tradition that continues today.

The Cleveland Society also was a pioneer in sub-contracting with private industry, and Vision Loss Resources continues that model today, operating Contract Production Services, which turns 100 percent of its profits back into services for Vision Loss Resources clients.

Vision Loss Resources' mission embraced client empowerment from its founding. The Cleveland Society was a strong influence, through a 1913 speech in Minneapolis by Mrs. E. B. Palmer, executive secretary of the society. That organization had a division that "deals with the organization of clubs to visit the blind in their homes and to help and encourage them." Vision Loss Resources follows that tradition through its mission "to create a community of service, skills and support for people with vision loss."

Hess Roise
Historical Consultants

Research by Penny Petersen and Charlene Roise, Hess, Roise and Company.

Historical research made possible by our sponsor, Hess, Roise and Company. We would like to thank Charlene Roise and Penny Petersen for their dedication and commitment to Vision Loss Resources. Our history is richer and far more accurate thanks to their involvement in our endeavors.

KAY TRAPP

A Brave New World

Alone in this strange place, I was in the exam chair listening as the retinal specialist laid out my diagnosis and prognosis. For some time I hadn't been able to see out of one eye, so first I went to my regular eye doctor. He was alarmed and said the problem was more serious than a pair of glasses could fix. He told me to see a specialist, and I was feeling scared.

The first specialist I went to told me the problem would go away on its own and to come back in three months. My sister was with me, and she thought it was nothing to be alarmed about. When my eye didn't improve in three months, I visited several different doctors and clinics, trying to find someone who could fix it. The doctors all said there was nothing they could do. I wondered if it would have helped to go to someone sooner, and I blamed myself.

Now I had taken the bus alone from Hastings to the Mayo Clinic in Rochester, where the retinal specialist told me I would end up completely blind. I was not expecting to hear this bleak news and tried to make sense of it. I cried all the way home on the bus, with no one to share the news with or help me put it into perspective.

At home, in the confines of my living room, I let my fingers do the walking through the phone book. I looked up "blindness and vision loss" and called a government agency, but that only left me frustrated. Next I called Vision Loss Resources. The people I talked to at Vision Loss Resources were very nice and left me feeling there was support and help for me. Soon Frank Alden visited me, followed by Ellen Morrow, and I felt I had a plan.

It has been several years since all this happened. Vision Loss Resources is still around, and I am still getting help and support from Ellen Morrow. And, through services at Vision Loss Resources, I am picking up an old passion of mine: writing. I no longer feel like a victim, and I still maintain a degree of independence.

Never say never. There is always hope.

VINCE ULSTAD

Living for a Purpose Much Greater Than Myself

Rarely do we ponder at length what unknown events may be waiting ahead for us on the road of life—at least, I certainly did not. Oh, I may have had an occasional fleeting thought, especially as I got older, as to whether I would avoid cancer or experience an early heart attack or stroke. But never once did I encounter the thought of becoming significantly disabled as the result of another person's decisions and actions. My world was joyfully full of family, friends, career, hobbies, and many other things that gave me a zest for life and for living. It was not my nature to spend time considering negative possibilities outside my normal decision-making process in typical life situations. Yet, now, after going through a very dramatic change and becoming a "disabled" person, I find great value in looking back to identify valuable factors that got me through this time and set me solidly on the remainder of my journey.

On Tuesday, June 2, 2009, I had taken an early morning drive to Carrington, North Dakota, for an all-day project review meeting. It was one of those magnificent, beautiful summer days on the wide-open prairie. As I drove along, the sun was coming up bright and clear, the wind was slight (always a treat in North Dakota!), and the meadowlarks along the roadsides were busy and loud. After the meeting concluded, I drove south and west to Steele, North Dakota, where I had recently established a field research project for my company. I worked until about 9:45 p.m. before packing up to begin the drive home. I stopped at the truck stop in Steele to fuel up my diesel Ford F-250 pickup and grabbed a cold sandwich and bottle of juice for the road.

Just a few minutes after getting on I-94, heading east for Fargo, I followed a semi truck up a hill with a curve near the top of it. As the truck slowed on the grade, I moved into the passing lane, but the curve, the hill, and the truck prevented me from seeing that an oncoming vehicle was in my lane, heading towards me. Our vehicles collided head-on at the top of the hill, both presumably going around 75 mph. Both the other driver and I were driving three-quarter-ton, full-size pickups. The other driver died at the scene. Highway patrol tests determined his blood alcohol content was just over three times the legal limit for driving.

While I have no memory of the accident, the emergency responders with whom I have visited since the accident have told me I was still conscious when they arrived at the scene. My left foot was broken and entangled in the foot pedals of the truck, and I was losing a significant amount of blood from severe wounds on the left side of my body. Apparently, regardless of how hard I struggled or how hard I wanted to save myself, I could not and required the help of others at the scene. It took about nine minutes for them to cut me out of my pickup. They put me in an ambulance and rushed me to MedCenter One Hospital in Bismarck, North Dakota. I arrived there shortly after midnight on June 3, 2009.

According to the emergency room doctors, my lungs and kidneys had already started to shut down. I continued to lose large quantities of blood. My left foot was broken in two places, my left leg was severely mangled, with significant muscle and nerve damage, and my pelvis was broken in eight locations. In addition, my jaw was broken and there were numerous fractures in my skull. Even though the airbag in the steering column had deployed, people who saw my pickup in the days following the accident reported that my head had hit the steering wheel so hard that it curved along the sides to fit my head.

The hospital reached my wife in Fargo shortly before 1 a.m. with the news that I had been in an accident, and they advised her to get to Bismarck as fast as she could. She and our youngest son arrived in Bismarck around 4:30 a.m. They told me that when they saw me, I was completely unrecognizable.

The doctors and nurses worked on me for twelve

hours straight. They had a difficult time identifying the source of all the internal bleeding. Thus, they had to wait four days before they could operate on me. I underwent several surgeries, including installation of a small titanium coil device in a major artery, where the bleeding would not stop, and facial reconstruction due to significant skull fracturing. This was likely the only time in my life when I could have put in my request to look like Robert Redford, John Wayne, or Matt Damon—and I had to sleep through it! Various titanium plates and screws were implanted in my hips and pelvis. Humpty Dumpty could have used the wonderful team of medical staff who took care of me! An external fixator was installed into and across my hips to lock the pelvis solid for three months. Moreover, my jaw was wired shut.

After a few weeks, the doctors realized I would likely survive physically. They began preparing my wife and children for a high probability that I would be blind and live the remainder of my life in a vegetative state (please, not in North Dakota!), due to the severe impact to my brain and the inevitability of traumatic brain injury. I was in a coma during these weeks. Exactly three weeks after the accident, I was airlifted to a long-term care hospital in Fargo. After two weeks, the doctors began bringing me out of the coma. During the week after Independence Day, I was fully out of the coma and found out, for the first time, what had happened over the past five weeks. I discovered I was completely and permanently blind due to irreversible damage to the optic nerve caused by the excessive and extended blood loss. The doctors told me that fifty-five units of blood were transfused before they were able to stabilize my condition. With the exception of some short-term memory difficulties, there is no evidence of loss of cognitive abilities, logical thought process, or reasonable thinking that can't be explained simply by the fact that I am Norwegian.

I spent nine weeks at Triumph Hospital in Fargo while my external wounds healed. On August 25, 2009, I was transferred to Elim Care Center in Fargo to begin physical and occupational therapy. I had lost thirty-five to forty pounds, my muscles had deteriorated, and I could not walk. Next, I was transferred to MeritCare Hospital's fulltime rehabilitation program to learn to walk again and to receive additional occupational therapy. Then, on November 19, I was discharged to return home, nearly six months after leaving home for that one-day business trip.

I received in-home physical and occupational therapy through the end of the year and began outpatient therapy in January 2010. During December 2009, and March, June, and September 2010, I spent multiple days at the North Dakota School for the Blind in Grand Forks, receiving training in braille, technology, orientation and mobility training, and independent living skills. The staff was, and continues to be, extremely encouraging and devoted to helping me maximize life again, almost to the point of their expecting miracles. One of the staff, who teaches independent living skills, is determined to get me proficient in the kitchen. He couldn't have done that when I had my eyesight!

Later, in October 2010, I developed a *Clostridium difficile* bacterial infection in my gastrointestinal tract. I had never heard of this somewhat common infection, which has symptoms on the human body identical to a nuclear laxative. It took three months to get that little bacteria under control, including an unexpected hospitalization for four days for dehydration.

Then, in March 2011, it became evident that an MRSA (methicillin-resistant Staph) bacterial infection had developed in my left hip, likely a consequence of the surgery of 2009 to implant the metal hardware. Between March and July, I underwent seven surgeries, multiple daily antibiotic IVs, and up to three daily bandage changes. Due to the frequency of daily medical attention, I lived in the hospital or at Elim Care Center from April through the week after Labor Day in September 2011.

In December that year, my wife and I, along with our two sons, enjoyed a two-week trip to Hawaii, a celebration of sorts for all that our family had been through during the previous three years. At this time, I was very excited about the future and God's plans for my life. But, in the summer of 2012, my wife informed me of her decision to file for divorce, which hit me harder than a two-by-four across the side of the head and has been, certainly, more painful than going blind. However, as with the accident, God continued to encourage me and remind me of his promises and presence. Thus, when 2013 began, I started to adjust to singleness and blindness, though I have a tremendous sense of serenity in the present and hope for the future.

As I have looked back on nearly four years, I can clearly identify several factors that helped me through a change in life I never could have imagined possible. First and foremost, I recognize that my identity and position as a follower of Jesus of Nazareth has provided the only foundation on which I could stand through such times. Second, at all key points during these experiences, top-notch medical personnel cared for me, including doctors, nurses, CNAs, therapists, emergency responders, and administration. For one who had been rarely sick, I took the healthcare community for granted and now have such a deep appreciation for them. Third, I received hundreds of visits, letters, phone calls, and emails.

In review, I noted that people posting notes on my Caring Bridge web page, emailing, calling, or writing represented five of the seven continents. Over 16,000 visits to the Caring Bridge site were recorded in the first few months and nearly 600 people visited my hospital room the first three months after I was returned to Fargo. The encouragement and prayers of so many people had a powerful medical effect on my body.

Now, I am able to live at home. Moreover, I am busy with speaking opportunities; involved in a start-up company, developing cloud-based software platforms for the smartphone and wireless Internet market; providing consultancy to an organization, Hope Centers for Children of Africa, on crop/food production in Africa; and working on various political projects. In many ways, I am enjoying life more now than ever. I certainly miss being able to see and visually enjoy the world around me, but I recognize that the busyness of life prior to becoming blind should not be equated with fullness of life. Every moment and experience in life is intended as part of a building process: selecting, cutting, fitting, and finishing us for use on behalf of purposes much greater than ourselves.

C. L. BODER

Blinders

When I was a child, sight seemed mysterious, like a butterfly or a fragile figurine.

I used to memorize parts of books and convince myself that I was reading them. When we were driving down the highway and my siblings pointed out other cars they saw, I said I could see them, too. My mother said I couldn't, but I didn't quite make the connection.

When I was four years old, I learned the meaning of the word *blind*. My mom and I were visiting two little blind boys who lived in Dodge Center, which is a little more than a shout from Rochester, where we lived at the time.

"Are you blind? Are you blind?" they asked excitedly as we swung on their swing set.

I didn't know what "blind" meant, so I didn't say anything. I was puzzled, though. The next day my mom explained that I was blind and that meant I couldn't see. While she was talking, I played with her coffee cup. What she was saying didn't really mean anything to me. I didn't get mad or cry. I didn't bang my head against the floor and scream, "That's not fair!" Happily, I now knew the meaning of the word *blind*. And that meant more to me than not being able to see.

Since I used my fingers instead of my eyes to explore my world, I thought of abstract concepts in terms of touch. For example, a minute was something you could hold in your hand. Another example: the sky wasn't vapor; it was bright, cold metal with Christmas-cookie stars.

Being blind didn't stop me from exploring the neighborhood. One day I came upon a hill made out of pebbles.

"Goody!" I said to myself. "I can play Candy Land!"

The small stones would make really fine pretend pieces of candy. But there was a surprise waiting for me at the top. I started climbing and—Ker-*plop*! I found myself at the bottom of a big hole. Dirt everywhere—and me, alone and forgotten.

"I will be here forever!" I thought sorrowfully, as I walked around my square prison. "They'll be having spaghetti for supper, and they'll talk about the little girl who got lost a long time ago. And I'll be here the whole time . . ."

Then I heard Mommy's pretty voice as she set down a ladder and helped me climb out of a hole that was going to be the basement of a house the neighbors were building. My heart sang with relief as I realized I wasn't going to be left there.

I have always been sensitive to atmosphere. Schools, for example, are weighted with the solemnity of students busy with concentration and learning; this is especially true of one-room country schools. Places where kids live are warm and happy. Cemeteries are usually peaceful.

The house where my maternal grandparents lived was full of joy and excitement. I loved going there when I was little, because it was like stepping smack-dab into Christmas or living inside a happy song.

After I started school, I used to torture my younger sisters by teasing them about their favorite colors. For instance, if they liked the color blue, I would state roughly, "Blue isn't pretty." They'd get upset and cry. It never occurred to them to scoff, "You can't even see it, dummy."

That seemed like the strangest thing of all.

ELAINE ZUZEK

Charlie

There's a new man in my life! His name is Charlie, and I met him almost two years ago. After nearly sixteen years of widowhood, I did not plan to or particularly want to become intimately involved with another man. Then I met Charlie after going to see a vitreoretinal specialist because my vision began to change.

After doing some tests, the doctor recommended a shot in one of my eyes to stop it from "leaking." The procedure went well. But, she said, I might see a bubble afterward that would likely go away. The next morning, I did see a bubble—in fact, I saw several, but I didn't become too concerned because the doctor had warned me, and I thought they would go away in a day or two. After I covered my affected eye, however, I saw a bubble in the other eye. This bubble had people in it—just headshots—like those in my high school yearbook. I also saw bugs, which morphed into familiar friends.

That afternoon I met Charlie. His official name is Charles Bonnet, and he is a syndrome that causes me to see the bubbles. The "scientific" explanation of this phenomenon is that my brain makes up what my eye can't see—in other words, I hallucinate.

Most of the time, the persons I see morph from one face to another—and I can identify some of them. They appear to be friends from high school. Ah, yes—Ruth morphs into Kathy—and they look as they looked in 1955. Sometimes, there's even a lovely background.

A few months after I realized I had this syndrome, I woke up to two bubbles—two smaller circles within the original circles—that soon morphed to make it appear as if "my people" wore glasses! If I'm farther than six inches away from others, "my people" pop over the faces of everyone I see. I don't dare talk to them—maybe I'm afraid they'll answer. At a choir concert, Charlie adds them to the choir. As I watch TV, they appear in a group somewhere on the screen.

Now these people are always with me. At times, I have to remind myself that if I want to see what people really look like when I meet them, I have to get in close to see their faces. I'm getting better at recognizing voices.

Fortunately, I have been blessed with great family and friends who know about "my people." Most of the time, Charlie is annoying rather than disabling, and I can laugh about him. But I don't think he's my friend, and I wish he would go away! I'm very grateful for the limited vision I have, though. And I'm an accomplished cusser, though I try not to cuss in public. But, if all else fails, cussing relieves my frustration.

DEBBIE WYGAL

Swimming in My Gene Pool: A Biologist Confronts Vision Loss and Heredity

"The role of the infinitely small is infinitely large."

— Louis Pasteur

My road to vision loss began purely by chance. As the egg cell in my mother's ovary began its maturation, the twenty-three pairs of chromosomes began to separate, in an intricate dance called meiosis. Her copy of chromosome 22, which carried a mutant gene, went into the egg cell that would be fertilized later by my father's sperm. It could have gone the other way. There was a fifty/fifty chance that I would get the chromosome 22 with the unaltered gene, but I was unlucky in the genetic lottery that day. And my twenty-nine-year-old mother had no clue that she was even carrying such a gene and had passed it along to me. Both of our lives would be profoundly altered.

In 2007, I learned we had an eye disease in my family called Sorsby fundus dystrophy (SFD). Sorsby is the last name of the British doctor who first discovered the disease in five English families in 1949. *Fundus* is a medical term referring to the base of any organ. In the eye, the fundus is the retina, a half-millimeter-thick layer lining the back of the eye. *Dystrophy*, another medical term, means "degeneration." I have retinal degeneration.

My disease is entry number 136900 in the "Online Mendelian Inheritance in Man" database, just in case you want to read all about it, which you probably don't. But I do and I can. Therein lies the rub. I am a biologist, a geneticist, who teaches courses in genetics and finds all the biology about my disease fascinating. At the same time, my vision loss has had a profound effect on how I live my life.

My maternal grandmother was the first person I remember having the disease. She was in her early sixties when her eyesight started to degenerate. I was about eleven years old at the time, and I remember my grandparents traveling to major medical centers all over the United States to find out what was wrong. No one knew. They simply didn't have the medical technology to analyze her eyes. She was told that it was probably the result of something she was exposed to as a child growing up in the hills of eastern Kentucky. The rest of us didn't think much more about it.

Then in the spring of 1984, when I was six months' pregnant with fraternal twin boys, my mother informed me that she had "Grandmother's disease." At age sixty-two, she was told she had "macular degeneration." My geneticist's mind quickly kicked into gear. This eye disease was hereditary and inherited as a dominant mutation. *Dominant* means that you only have to inherit one bad copy of the gene to get the disease. My risk of inheriting the gene was now at 50 percent, and each of my unborn children thus had a 25 percent risk.

This is an adult-onset disease, meaning that although you inherit the gene or genes at conception, the symptoms don't appear until adulthood. For SFD, the average age is forty-five to fifty years old. It appeared that in my family the average age of onset was early sixties. When my mother's symptoms appeared, I was thirty-two and sixty seemed a long way off in my future. So imagine my surprise when, at forty-six, I noticed symptoms of the disease in myself.

I will never forget that day. I had been diligent about seeing an ophthalmologist once a year. "Your retinas look fine," she told me repeatedly. I also used an Amsler eye grid somewhat regularly. The grid has a series of intersecting lines with a dark circle at the middle. You cover one eye and look at the grid. If the lines appear wavy, your central vision may be affected. As it turns out, I didn't need the Amsler grid. One afternoon when I was teaching lab, a student asked me to look at a graph she had drawn. I looked and noticed that the lines were not straight but wavy. "Oh no," I thought and immediately made an appointment with my eye doctor. Several days later, she examined me and said that my retinas looked fine, but maybe the retinal specialist should come down to take a look. He did and saw many lesions called *drusen* on the macula of both eyes. The macula is the center of the retina and the area involved in seeing detail, such as print on a page or recognizing faces. Drusen are lesions on the retina containing cellular debris, an indicator of damage or degeneration. My journey had begun.

I was pulled in many directions after my diagnosis. Could I continue in my career as a professor of biology? I love my work, but it involves a lot of reading, computer work, and laboratory manipulations. What about my love for reading as a leisure activity? Could I still do it? And what was this disease my family had? It wasn't simple age-related macular degeneration (AMD), the leading cause of vision loss in the United States, the prevalence of which sharply increases after age seventy. (It is predicted that four million Americans will have AMD by the year 2030.)

Over the next few years, as my disease progressed, I found myself squinting at the computer screen, looking for large-print text, and needing emotional support for the loss I was experiencing. I thought that there must be technology that could help me, but I didn't know where to find it or what, specifically, I needed. I sought help from my university, which appeared to have nothing in place for faculty with disabilities. They even told the office for students with disabilities not to work with me. Although they gave me money to buy the equipment I needed, they offered no support for its use after I got it. I looked for a support group. I asked my retinal specialist about organizations that helped people with vision loss, but he didn't know of any.

My introduction to Vision Loss Resources came purely by chance. My partner's mother, who was living in an assisted living facility and had vision loss, was scheduled for a visit from a community service person from Vision Loss Resources. I decided to sit in on the visit to see what I might learn. Meeting Ellen Morrow that day changed my life. I was amazed to learn about all that the organization did, and I was elated when she said, "I think I have a support group you might like." In the years since, I have become very involved in the organization, both receiving services and giving back as a member of the board of directors, an empowering situation all around.

But what disease did my family have? I needed to know both as a scientist and as a parent, who might have passed the gene to her sons, each of whom now had a 50 percent chance of getting the disease. A retinal specialist at the University of Minnesota examined my eyes and concluded that it might be one of two diseases, and the only way to be certain was to do genetic testing. She told me to see Dr. Ed Stone, a retinal doctor at the University of Iowa who specialized in hereditary retinal diseases.

I went to Iowa City and spent a day participating in many tests. At the end of that day, Dr. Stone told me that he was 99 percent certain that I had Sorsby fundus dystrophy, but only a genetic test would confirm it. He told me that the mutant gene was on the long arm of chromosome 22. The gene is called TIMP-3, and it carries the information for cells to make a protein called "tissue inhibitor of metalloproteinase 3." Dr. Stone said that the mutations in the TIMP-3 gene in most people with SFD clustered in a region of the gene called exon 5. Mutations are changes in the bases (As, Cs, Ts, and Gs) that make up the sequence of DNA. Because genes carry the information to make proteins, a change in a gene's base sequence can change the sequence of the amino acids in the corresponding protein, and the protein may be reduced in function or be completely nonfunctional. In SFD, the altered TIMP-3 protein forms clumps in the retina and is resistant to degradation by other proteins that control its amount.

I gladly gave up a vial of blood for genetic testing. The white blood cells in the blood would be isolated and the DNA extracted for analysis. I left the University of Iowa that day excited by the prospect of my genetic test results, but sad because my vision continued to deteriorate and I had to stop driving. That was six years ago, and I have not driven since.

No longer being able to drive is a major loss of independence. I am always trying to figure out how to get where I want to go. I've gotten to know the Yellow Cab drivers in my area and purchased a three-wheeled recumbent bike by which I commute to work when the Minnesota weather will allow. Once again, Vision Loss Resources helped me out, doing the paperwork required to use Metro Mobility, a transit service for people with disabilities.

As for my genetic test, the results came back negative. I did not have a mutation in exon 5 of the TIMP-3 gene. Dr. Stone explained that his lab had only analyzed exon 5 of my gene, and they were now going to look at the rest of my gene. Sure enough, they found a single base change in exon 1, substituting an amino acid called cysteine for the normal one, lysine. This was the first time his lab had encountered this mutation. My geneticist's brain was excited at the prospect of a novel mutation—why, maybe my gene would be mentioned in a paper in a scientific journal! Meanwhile, my retinal cells continued to degenerate. I could not drive, could not read text, could not see faces clearly, and had 20/200 vision in one eye and 20/400 in the other. A change of one base pair in a tiny region of my DNA had led to a major impact on my life. Therefore, the quote at the beginning of this essay—"the role of the infinitely small is infinitely large"—really applies here. Louis Pasteur was referring to microorganisms, but the analogy is apt.

I use my eye disease as a teaching tool in my classes, especially genetics. The disease is a great example of some basic concepts in genetics—the relationship of genes to proteins, the inheritance pattern of a dominant trait—but far more important, I put a human face on the disease. I have this vision loss, but I can still teach this class, grade student papers, and be a scholar. Disabled does not mean unable or incompetent or dumb.

The grief associated with vision loss is ongoing. There are good days and bad days—days when I can laugh at having eaten moldy bread because I didn't see the mold, and days when I quite simply feel sorry for myself and wish everyone could experience the world briefly as I do because maybe then they would be more understanding. There are days when I want to smack the bus driver with my white cane because he didn't help me navigate the stairs onto the bus. And every day, I think of my mother, grandmother, and great uncle, who all had this disease, and I wish they had known what it was. I especially think of my twenty-nine-year-old fraternal twin sons, and I hope that on the day of their conception, the copies of chromosome 22 with the "bad" TIMP-3 gene did not go into my eggs. I fervently wish them success in the genetic lottery.

TARA ARLENE INNMON

Painting Heaven

I.
As a baby I saw the world through operated eyes.
The light hurt; I wasn't going blind then.
There was a threat;
The doorway of vision
could be slammed shut at any time.

In school I sat at my desk
staring hard while drawing what I saw around me:
profiles, backs of heads, hands:
Photographs I thought I could save.

My mother said I was good
So I painted landscapes for relatives.

Then I put aside my art.
It seemed mechanical.
It was what my mother wanted.

II.
My mother is dead.
I start again as the door begins to close,
painting with my nose too close to the canvas,
neck aching.

I go outside to paint,
it looks like a little girl's heaven.
I walk on clouds; my feet disappear,
sunk in billows of shimmering gray and white.
Light glows from dark gray
sending out rays of soft white arms
tinted yellow or maybe pink,
maybe near cloud blue.
Light bounces from objects I don't see.
Cars driving by are chariots of streaming light
and I walk through the essence of things.
My heart fills just as it used to
watching the sunset.
But where will I find joy
if I lose the light?

III.
My mind creates checkerboard squares where the
    gaps are.
Like the alphabet blocks I learned as a little girl
to place in a row close enough
so another one can go on top
        and another
higher,
        higher
until collapse.

CYNTHIA MCFADDEN
Becoming Legally Blind

W hy can't I see?" I mumbled under my breath. *"Why can't I see?"* I nearly screamed internally as I traveled from Sioux Falls, South Dakota, to Burnsville, Minnesota. I had taken this trip many, many times to visit my sister, Laurie. Why did it take eight hours to drive home instead of the usual four hours?

After I spent the night at Laurie's, I woke up early that Sunday morning and ate a quick breakfast. Then I said goodbye to Laurie and her husband, Darvin, and headed to my car. The air was February South Dakota crisp; it frosted the inside of my nose, adding crystals to my nostril hair. I had to scrape the frosty windows and windshield, and clear snow off the car. As I scraped the windows, I felt apprehensive about the trip. I hadn't told anyone about my decreased vision, and I don't really think I had fully comprehended that I was losing my sight.

As I drove out of town, I thought I'd take a new route by the airport but became lost, seeing unfamiliar places and buildings. I knew I had to go north and east, so I kept driving until I found I-90 and headed east to Minnesota.

Later, I came to Worthington, Minnesota, and

stopped at a car wash. I tried to read the instructions on the sign, but I became confused because I couldn't see. Snow was piled up around the car—little hills of snow that reminded me of how my siblings and I loved to climb hills and gather snow balls to throw at each other when we were young.

"Why can't I *see*?" I asked myself over and over. I got out of the car and went up to the sign, squinting to read the words. Then I got back into the car and waited in line to go into the car wash. Car after car came up behind me, waited, and then moved over to the other car wash station. In a daze, I watched, feeling as if I were in limbo. My mind seemed like a jigsaw puzzle with pieces stuck in the wrong places. As I sat there, I began to feel cold. "*Snap out of it,*" I told myself. "*Grow up! Someone can help you get your car washed.*"

I trudged to the gas station, found help with the car wash, and began my journey again. As I drove, I could see the white lines on the right-hand side of the road. When I turned my head, I could see the middle lines. I traveled, watching those lines until I came to a town with an Applebee's restaurant. I stopped to rest and gather my wits. It took nearly two hours for me to decompress.

Later, I headed back toward the interstate. When I came to the on ramp, I thought I was going in the right direction but soon realized I was on the wrong ramp, going against traffic.

"*Oh no!*" I thought. I stopped and sat there, trying to figure out what to do next.

I decided to back up. No cars were coming. Thank the Lord, no cars were coming. No accidents, no deaths, no mangled bodies, no wrecked cars. I prayed my thanks that others and I had been saved from my dangerous trek. During that ordeal, my body had tensed up, but as the morning extended into a bright, clear Minnesota day, my body relaxed. I felt the strain on my eyes, though, as I struggled to keep the car on the road between the lines. My head began to throb with pain.

Eventually, my tires crunched on the snow-pitted driveway as I drove into my apartment complex. I sighed with relief, releasing my white-knuckled hands from the steering wheel. After I parked, I just sat there, wondering how in the world I had made it home in one piece. I recalled that years earlier while driving in a snowstorm, I couldn't see a thing, so I had stopped. A semi-truck rushed passed me, driving on the other side of the road. I believed then, as I do now, that God spared my life so I could do good things for humanity.

One day, I finally discovered why I couldn't see. Over the course of twenty years, a brain tumor called a meningioma had grown on my frontal lobe, damaging my optic nerve and causing the gradual loss of vision. While I haven't lost all of my sight, I am now legally blind.

PAMELA R. FLETCHER

Things Not Seen

After he graduated from high school, my close childhood friend Dwayne enlisted in the army. One day, several years later, while serving under Commander-in-Chief Reagan, Dwayne's world went black. Upon returning home, he told my mother he thought the lights had gone out; he expected them to come on again, but he couldn't flip the switch. Somehow, he had landed in perpetual darkness. Hearing his story, I wondered how he could be so unlucky at such a young age. Dwayne eventually became wheelchair bound, and soon afterward he died—at least that's what I recall.

The truth is, upon further recollection, I don't remember how long he lived after he lost his sight. The truth is that I soon forgot about him because I couldn't bear to see him gain weight and become helpless—so unlike Rabbit, his former self. Sleek Rabbit had both fast feet and quick wit. He and I ran track in school—he would tease me mercilessly about my funny gait, and I would chase him fiercely, only making him laugh harder.

After he became blind, his jokes fell flat, no longer corny and clever. They became desperate attempts to keep me close so I wouldn't just pop in and out of his bedroom like our friends, who seldom visited. I had a good excuse not to visit often because I had left California for Minnesota and saw him only when I visited family and friends during school breaks. I don't recall when I stopped visiting him. I kept up with him by way of my mother and my aunt, his neighbor. I stuffed my guilt deep inside, running away from him rather than running after him. When I heard he had died, I felt bewildered and sad. I never expected him to die before I'd see him again. I don't recall what I was doing when Mrs. Durley buried Dwayne, her eldest son. No doubt, I was preoccupied with living fast and seeing the world, taking my life and eyes for granted.

One day, in the winter of 2013, while I was looking in the bathroom mirror, the light disappeared and the room turned black. I suddenly remembered Dwayne telling my mother that he had gone blind within seconds. Frantically, I felt for the light switch and fiddled with it, sweating profusely until I got it to turn back on. A few minutes earlier, when the light had gone out, I feared that I had gone blind in my right eye, which would render me completely blind. I reacted drastically, eventually feeling silly, for I knew about the malfunctioning light and had intended to repair it each time it stopped working, which was every day. But my sudden memory of Dwayne transported me from composure to shifting states of despair and grief. I slumped over the bathroom sink as tears filled my eyes, dimming my already diminished right eye, while I mourned Dwayne's death and my blind left eye.

In the early 1990s, I found out I had ocular hypertension, which meant that the pressure in my eyes was beyond the normal range, creating an increased risk of my contracting glaucoma. Glaucoma is an eye disease that damages the optic nerves in a person's eyes, eventually causing blindness if the ocular pressures aren't controlled with medication. I discovered that I was at high risk for getting this disease because my mother and sister had been diagnosed with it, I'm African American, and I'm nearsighted. So, I began to undergo frequent eye exams and to use eyedrops daily. I didn't think much about my condition, because the medicine kept the ocular pressures under control for fifteen years.

One day, however, during an eye examination, the ophthalmologist discovered that the ocular pressures in my eyes had risen to dangerous levels. After a process of eliminating potential reasons for the rise, he asked me if I was using steroids. "What? Why would I use steroids?" I answered incredulously. When he explained that they could be in a cosmetic product, I recalled that two weeks earlier I had begun using a prescriptive cream I had gotten from a dermatologist. The ophthalmologist urged me to stop using it, which I did immediately. A week later, when I returned for a follow-up appointment, he found that my ocular pressures had returned to their normal state. I learned then that I was a steroid responder, and I assumed he had documented the incident in my file.

In the summer of 2010, the ophthalmologist advised pre-emptive surgery to prevent my ocular pressures from climbing and to ensure that my eyes would be healthy in the future.

The following spring, I decided to undergo surgery, beginning with the weaker eye, my left one. After three consultations, I chose what was considered a less invasive procedure than the other options, which the ophthalmologist performed. During the post-op appointment with him, I asked about each prescription he had prescribed, and he identified one of them as a steroid. Feeling alarmed, I questioned why he had prescribed it, given my previous response to steroids. He stated that temporary, carefully monitored usage of such a small amount wouldn't be harmful and that I'd experience less pain and would heal faster. His explanation seemed reasonable, so I used it along with the other prescriptions. But, when I woke up two days later, I couldn't see out of my left eye. During the night I had worn a patch, but I thought that somehow I must have gotten something in my eye or rubbed it too hard as I slept. Throughout the day, the vision in my left eye came and went, and I grew anxious and afraid. The next morning I rushed to the doctor's office for an emergency appointment. Shortly afterward, I discovered that I was going blind in my left eye and that the optic nerve in my right eye, which had yet to undergo surgery, was now damaged. In a panic, the ophthalmologist immediately called one of the University of Minnesota eye surgeons and then sent me speeding down Highway 394 East for emergency surgery at the University hospital to save my sight. As I drove, I could only pray, "Please, God, help me to see so I can get there right away."

March 28, 2011, the day of that fateful surgery, began the start of my surreal existence. My mother, a registered nurse, began to wonder how the optic nerves in both my eyes got damaged. "You're having a systemic reaction to something," she said. And she was right. It turned out that the prescribed steroid for my left eye wasn't the culprit. After enduring six weeks of my persistent questions, a University of Minnesota glaucoma specialist, who had performed the subsequent eye surgeries, eventually revealed to me that as a matter of course, during the procedure, her colleague had injected a steroid cocktail in my left eye to aid its recovery. *What?* I felt stunned and angry. How could he have done this, especially after he had advised me a few years earlier to stop using a cream containing a steroid because it caused my ocular pressures to rise to dangerous levels? Had he forgotten to document the incident? Feeling vulnerable and dismayed, I wondered how I could ever trust any doctor again. Yet I soon realized that if I focused on feeling powerless, I wouldn't be able to concentrate on regaining my sight, so I began to pray to God to heal me.

I couldn't bear to think about my inability to see again, for I enjoyed making a living as an English professor, an editor, and a writer. I wanted so badly to hold on to my livelihood and independence. But I began to wonder how long I could last in the classroom, where, suddenly, I could barely see the faces of my students. To cover the wild look of my red eyes, I began to wear shades, which bothered some of the students, and they later complained in their course evaluations. I wanted to tell them what I was going through, but I felt too vulnerable and afraid. Instead, I pretended that everything was normal, while I could no longer write on the board, and I had to rely on some students to read the course materials out loud because I couldn't read them. Outside the classroom, I spent two to three times longer grading papers, and I could barely read online to check my email.

By mid-August 2012, I'd had two surgeries on my left eye and one on my right eye. During the glaucoma procedure on both the right and left eyes, the surgeon had inserted a Baerveldt valve implant and graft (or a tube shunt) in them to control the ocular pressure so I could retain my low vision. Meanwhile, my life changed daily, as my sight grew dimmer and dimmer. In the fall of 2012, I went from seeing double to not being able to see well at all, especially in wet weather. Soon, I realized that I could no longer see out of my left eye. During the winter of 2013, I requested rides from friends and learned to take the bus to and from work. When I thought things could get no worse, I began slipping and falling because I'd lost my depth perception. Yet, I told myself, "You can't stop moving."

I had to move slowly along the icy sidewalks and roads so I wouldn't fall. One day a colleague said she didn't recognize me because my gait had changed. She said I walked like an old woman. When I tried to tell her and others how my life had been altered, they didn't believe me because I "didn't look like a real blind person." While my mother couldn't see my physical difference, she could tell over the phone that I had changed. I would hear her weeping, but I told myself, "Don't you cry." I did cry, but only to God in my prayers. And I kept moving.

Someone told me to use a cane. My sister advised me to ride Metro Mobility. "You're disabled now," she declared.

Her chilling words brought to mind images of Dwayne sitting in his wheelchair. My inability to move and function like I had before enabled me to understand and imagine what he might have felt when others forgot about or misunderstood him, as the world spun around him at a dizzying speed.

Before I'd admit to myself that I was disabled, I decided to make a trip to the Mayo Clinic during my upcoming summer break. In the meantime, I went for a routine visual field exam to check my overall sight. The ophthalmologist, the one who had inserted the tube shunts in both my eyes, announced good news. She explained that although my left eye had developed a thick membrane, laser surgery would remove it.

"Are you saying I will see again?"

"Yes," she nodded, smiling.

I was skeptical. After all I'd gone through, I didn't feel I could trust her.

"What about the steroids? You know I can't use them. You said so yourself," I countered.

"That was before your eyes healed from the surgeries. You're okay now. And, with those shunts in your eyes, you're now the bionic woman, my dear. Steroids won't harm you anymore."

Today, nearly a year after the laser surgery, I've adjusted to having low vision in both eyes, a strange sensation, as if I'm looking at the world through a veil. But I can now walk without falling and move down stairs without tripping, and I can drive at night and read most material, online or printed. Each morning when I awake, I remind myself that the laser surgery was real, not a dream, and I thank God that I can see again, with both eyes. Even though I can see, however, I've learned not to rely on sight but on faith. As the writer of Hebrews 11:1 declares, "Now faith is the substance of things hoped for, the evidence of things not seen." I don't know what tomorrow holds, but I do know that my faith in God will hold me together.

CAROL ALPERIN

Snowstorm

By the summer of 1959, when I was twelve years old and about to enter seventh grade, I was experiencing what I called "the slow shutter." It was as if a camera shutter would start to close at one side of my eye, usually the left side, and as it moved to the right, my vision would slowly disappear. It felt as if I could take the shutter's edge and peel it away, but of course I couldn't. When the shutter started to close, I could be doing anything: riding a bike, roller-skating, crossing a street, or reciting in front of the class. I also had what I named "frosted glass" or "snowstorm vision" then too, when the shutter would gradually open up again and my vision would come back, blurry and clouded. The snowstorm could last from one to three days; it was very annoying and also frightening.

School became a nightmare that year. Our small town had only one school building for all twelve grades, and no kindergarten. The fifth and sixth grades were in the basement; the ground floor went from first to fourth grades; and the seventh through twelfth grades were on the second floor. The wider and safer front stairway was off-limits to high school students, leaving only the darker, steeper, more crowded stairway to be used by older students. Using that stairway was terrifying for me, as I was only about sixty pounds and four and a half feet tall, and it made me want to avoid school altogether. I became a truant. The superintendent came to my house to get me twice, until my teachers and I worked out a better way for me to get to my classes.

The first day of school in the new year, January 1960, came after a huge snowfall. Snow flurries started again that afternoon. I had an after-school activity that day; I believe it was Girl Scouts. My sixth-hour class was English, and my seventh hour was study hall. In English class the girl who sat in front was a platinum blonde, a light color like the color of my foggy vision. I could see denser things like bodies then, but faces and facial features were just a blur. I stared at my friend's hair because it seemed like a puffball, then asked her if she had cut it. She turned and said, "No more ponytail."

I spent study hall thinking and worrying about the snowstorm, my vision, and what it would be like trying to walk home with my vision as it was. When my after-school meeting was finished, it was time to go home. The other girls walked in different directions. I went south on what was supposed to have been the blacktop road that went north and south crossing Highway 55. The first street I reached had a sidewalk, but it was unshoveled so I crossed, thinking I could walk along the curb. I got to the next street and crossed that. This street had the Presbyterian church with a little, short sidewalk in front of it. I thought I could travel along that street and follow the pile the snowplow had made. All of a sudden I hit snow, deep enough in places to reach my waist. I stopped to listen and heard a thick and muffled sound, making any sense of direction impossible. Frightened, I waited, and finally heard the sound of a car. I knew it was too far away for me to be close to the street. By mistake, I had walked into the church's vacant lot.

Forcing my way through the deep, untracked snow, I did eventually find the snowbank made by the plow. By this time it was totally dark, and I kept following the bank until I saw some vague light through the fog. Thinking I had gone far enough, I turned left and walked into the deep snow of the ditch before our driveway. This time I knew where I was, so I waded through the waist-deep snow until I reached our house. What a relief to find those steps! That four-block walk home had taken me almost forty minutes to accomplish.

I must've been already doing many things by touch then, especially familiar things that were routines and could be done automatically. After supper that evening, while my mother was preparing to wash dishes, I sewed the last button on my home ec project. I realized then that I was working by touch only. I looked over to where the lamp was and saw only a very large fluffy sun. I finished my sewing, put my things away, and went to dry dishes.

"Mom," I said quietly, "I don't think my sight will come back this time." Of course she began to cry. I set down the dish and the dishtowel and put my arms around her. "Mom, I don't know what God's plans are, what he has in store for me, but he does have plans for me." I hugged her tighter. "Oh Mom," I said, "I was put on this earth for a reason. I might not ever know what the reason is, but God does."

I was right. After that day I only saw shadows and some bright objects such as aluminum foil.

KATHY D'AVIA

Kathy's Story

L et me start with when I lost my vision. I guess I should tell you that I am a dwarf, 4 feet 3 inches tall. On April 13, 1999, I went into the hospital to have back surgery. The surgery lasted thirteen hours, and five gallons of fluid were put in me. I was swollen so badly you couldn't tell where my nose was.

The next morning, when the nurse was taking my vital signs, I asked what time it was and she said "six a.m." As I lay in the dark, I told her I was concerned about missing the soap opera *Days of Our Lives*, which came on at noon, then went back to sleep.

I dozed in and out of sleep all day, drugged with morphine, and felt fairly good. It was dark, but I didn't realize anything was wrong. When my daughter visited after dinner, I asked her to read to me. She got a magazine, started reading, and asked if I wanted to look at the pictures. I said I didn't know how she could read because it was so dark in the room. She turned on a light and asked if that was better. I told her I couldn't see anything. Nervous, she got the nurse, who came and checked my eyes: they were dilated and the pupils did not get smaller when she shone a light on them.

Soon the entire surgical team arrived, and I was

moved to the MRI room. Doctors took the pictures out of the MRI machine as soon as they were printed and even had a radiologist who works with little people come in. At two a.m., the main doctor told my family that the team didn't know what caused my blindness nor if I would regain my vision. The next morning a specialist, who did not have good bedside manner, told me I might gain a little vision in the next couple of days, but he didn't think that would happen. In fact, the blood supply to my optic nerves had been cut off, and that had caused my blindness. When my daughter and I were alone, she put her forehead on mine and we both had tears running down our cheeks.

When it was time to leave the hospital and go to a rehabilitation center, I wore a plastic body cast that went from my shoulders down to the top of my legs. It opened in the front and was very uncomfortable. The rehab nurses didn't seem to know what to do with me, but when the weekend was over and the regular staff returned, I was moved to a private room and things went better. After six weeks, I was able to go home and I got around without any problems.

At home, realizing I would be blind for the rest of my life, I decided I had two choices. One was to be an angry dwarf and expect to be taken care of. The second choice was to learn to live like a blind person. I decided at that point to learn how to live like a blind person and got in touch with Vision Loss Resources.

Three months after the surgery, my doctor gave

me a work release that stated I could go back to work for two hours a day. Before the surgery I had worked at General Mills; I knew I wasn't ready to return and that General Mills would not be ready for me. Both my supervisor and the General Mills doctor had called me in the rehab center to tell me I was eligible for Social Security disability benefits and long-term disability insurance. Each time I told them I was coming back to work—maybe not in three months, but I was coming back.

A couple of years before, I had worked on a project to convert all of General Mills onto the same computer program. That fall after my surgery, General Mills was going to upgrade the computer system and the same team was going to work on it. My team colleagues said that they would not work on the new system if I didn't come back to do accounts receivable. "We don't care if she just sits there," they said. "We want her brain!"

I eventually did go back to work at General Mills. A General Mills commuter van picked me up at home, dropped me off in the parking ramp of the Interchange Building across the highway from the company, then picked me up there at the end of the day. Vision Loss Resources gave me mobility training so that I could manage on my own, taking the elevator to the ninth floor and getting around in my department. One afternoon, at the close of day, I took the wrong elevator, got off, and turned to the left. Using a white cane and tapping my way, all of a sudden I felt a large plant. I knew there was no plant on my way to the parking ramp. A lady asked if I needed help. "Yes," I said, "I am looking for the parking ramp." She was quiet for some time and then asked, "Are you going to drive?" "No," I told her, "I am getting picked up there." If I had put on my smarty pants, I might have said, "No, I am going to get on my motorcycle."

It has been fourteen years since I lost my vision, and I have had all sorts of experiences I could write about: four back surgeries, one neck surgery, and breast cancer. Now I live in an assisted living facility, where I am safe and get the help I need. I have lost some of my independence, but I keep fighting for the independence I still have. Normally I find my way to my chair in the dining room without assistance. On occasion, when I am listening to conversations or talking, I move in the wrong direction and other residents give me directions. I snap at them that I'll ask for help when I need it! In the beginning they would grab my arm to pull me around or put their hands on my walker to guide me. I have growled enough for them to know now not to touch me or my walker.

DIANA VANASSE

Driving Miss Maddy

In the past, driving was one of my favorite things to do. I loved being able to hop into my car and go to McDonald's, to my friends, to run to the store because I needed one more thing to complete dinner, to go to the beach, and most of all, to see my grandchildren play a game, swim, sing, dance, and all the fun things grandchildren do. I loved the freedom driving gave me.

The last time I drove my car, my granddaughter, Maddy, was sitting in the back in her car seat. We decided to go shopping. I loved taking Maddy with me wherever I went: to the movies, to restaurants, and to the mall.

On a beautiful summer day in Duluth, we drove to the mall. The sun was shining and the sky was baby blue, without a cloud in sight. I drove up a steep hill as we chatted happily. Suddenly Maddy yelled, "Oh Grandma!" in a very scared voice. I was driving fast while the driver in front of me was not, so I was heading right for the trunk of the car at a fast pace. I had no idea I was that close to it because my depth perception had become poor, which I had not yet admitted to myself. I had about one second to decide what to do. There was a car on my left, so I could not change lanes, and the car in front of me was not gaining speed. I slammed on my brakes, but I kept getting closer to the car in front of me. Fortunately, I saw a right-turn lane next to me. Quickly, I jerked the steering wheel and we flew to the right, balancing on two wheels. We landed on all four wheels without rolling over. Then, I slid around the corner, flew out of my car, grabbed my lovely granddaughter out of her car seat, collapsed on the ground, and cried my eyes out.

After recovering from my terrifying ordeal, I put Maddy back into her seat and drove nervously to McDonald's to get her a happy meal. Pretending that nothing had happened, I took her home, kissed her goodbye, and told her she didn't need to tell her mommy about our adventure.

Then I drove home, put my car in the garage, and never drove again. I finally had to admit to myself that it was not safe for me to drive. Now, my children don't have to tell me that I should not drive anymore.

TARA ARLENE INNMON

It's Because of the Drought That I Can't See

Pale yellow straw grass
looks the same as the sidewalk,
the same as everything:
that's why I can't see.
Where did the dark green go
that outlined a white path for me?
This is a hard drought.

The door to the SuperValu
seems to have disappeared into a gray and brick fog
but I hear footsteps, the whoosh of the door opening
and I know the way through
and I am inside and I am OK.

Last summer when it was green,
I went to the Minneapolis Society for the Blind
for their rehab program in case I lost more vision.
An instructor told me I must use a white cane
to identify to others that I couldn't see well.
So I began to practice with a cane—
but now I have to practice with it all the time.

That autumn on the bus
to and from the rehab center
I stared out the window
at an unusually dark and foggy fall.
One of those mornings
I let myself know that my sight was going.

My throat tight when I got off the bus,
I went straight to the rehab exercise room,
a small room with a treadmill
and a braille writer on the table.
I let tears and sobs out.

I didn't want to lose more vision!
I needed to paint pictures of what I saw.
A fellow student, Tom, entered the room.
I tried to stop crying
as I said hi and rolled paper into the braille writer.
I didn't fool him.
He asked what was wrong
so kindly that the tears came even harder.
He said that he had cried a lot too at the beginning
but now, after learning how to be independent
he was excited about his new life.
And that he was sure that some day
I would feel better about being blind.

I quit the program soon after that:
I needed time to paint
before it was too late.
That is what I do.
No doctor has told me that I am permanently losing
   my eyesight
and until I hear that . . .

I began to ride my bicycle only on the sidewalk;
This spring I ran into a child's Big Wheel.
My bike now sits in the garage
waiting for the drought to end
for I *will* ride my bike again!
Nobody is taking that away from me!

Last night, turning around
after putting something on my dresser,
I saw black in front of me.
Thinking I must be facing the darkened living room
with my back against the dresser,
I slowly walked forward,
waiting to feel the living room carpet on my bare feet.
Instead my knee hit the bed.

Where was the pale light that came through the
    curtains?
Pulling it aside,
I looked out at the hot, dark summer night.
A streetlight must have burned out.
Maybe it's connected to the drought.
I hope they put it in soon so I can see again.
When I pull out my food stamps at the SuperValu,
the cashier asks, "Can I help you?"
I can see my food stamps.
No one has ever asked me that before.
Do I look like I'm blind?

KATE GRATHWOL

Growing into Vision

I am the fifth of six children born into a family of dark-haired Irish. The first thing the nurse said to my mother was that I had beautiful, long, blonde hair. "Blonde hair?" my mother asked. You see, all my siblings and my parents were beautiful, black-haired Irish. Off I went with my parents to our lively, happy home. I had a lot of fun playing with my three brothers and two sisters, a whole playground of kids all under the same roof as I was.

As I grew up, it became apparent that I had a vision problem. No one thought too much about it, because both my parents wore glasses and we assumed that I, too, would one day wear glasses. It turned out, though, to be more complicated than that. To prepare to go to kindergarten, I went with my mother to the local optometrist, who promptly referred my mother to an ophthalmologist. He took one look at my eyes and told my mother that I was an albino, that I would never graduate from high school, thread a needle, drive a car, or go on to higher education. I would, however, make a nice housewife.

This news did not go over well with my mother, an educated, professional woman who had high ambitions for her children. She took me to the University of Minnesota to learn more about albinism: what it was, what it meant, and what, if anything, could be done about it. As it turned out, we learned quite a lot, and this is where the story gets interesting. Albinism is genetic, meaning it is passed on through the genes. Neither of my parents nor none of their ancestors were albino. My mother, a historian, already had done quite a bit of genealogy on her family. An albino relative certainly would have stood out, as I did. Yet, at the University of Minnesota genetics labs, where a lot of research on albinism was being done at the time, the geneticists determined that both of my parents' ancestors had emigrated from County Cork, Ireland, where a high incidence of albinism occurred. Therefore, each of my parents likely had a slight weakness in a gene, which resulted in my becoming an albino. Among the many variations of albinism, there is tyrosinase positive, which I discovered I had. Being tyrosinase positive means I have blue eyes and some pigment. As a child I had less pigment than I do now, and subsequently my vision was worse then than it is now.

The geneticists tested me for albinism by taking my almost snow-white hair and comparing it to the hair of one of my brothers and one of my sisters. When the scientists put my hair in the tyrosinase, it turned dark brown and looked just like my siblings' hair. Ah, but for a weak gene on both sides of my parents' ancestors, I would have had beautiful dark brown or auburn hair, and normal vision. Here I was, a child with low vision, a pack of siblings to keep up with, and a mother who was not going to let her daughter be slowed down by a little thing like legal blindness!

She and everyone else treated me like they treated all the other kids. I didn't get extra strikes at baseball and four square, though I wasn't very good. And I learned to ride a bike as well. I do remember wondering how on earth I ran into the neighbors' 1955 Chevrolet (aqua and white). It was as big as a barn. I couldn't see everything, and there were mysteries much too big for me to solve. I just bumped along with all the other kids, just doing what they did.

When I was in kindergarten, the school officials tested my vision to determine if I should go down to the State School for the Blind in Faribault, Minnesota. After a half day of testing and interviewing, they decided I probably would do just fine in the public schools with the support of my siblings, rather than be on my own in Faribault. So I went to grade school and high school with all my siblings.

The interesting thing about being tyrosinase positive is that there's a high chance of one building up more and more melanin, the active ingredient in pigment, so one's hair could get a little darker and one's eyesight could improve. Amazingly, that's exactly what happened. The summer between sixth and seventh grades, between my twelfth and thirteenth birthdays (I was born in the fall), my vision really improved. I spent the whole summer on our front porch reading the good books my mother, a librarian, recommended. I remember thinking, "Now I'm going to read all the books I couldn't read when I was younger because reading was just too much work." Eventually, as I mowed through book after book after book, I realized that I no longer had to work so hard to read. Because my vision had improved since I was in grade school, I had an easier time getting through high school. I even got my driver's license, miracle of miracles. Although I don't have perfect vision, I have near-normal vision, and it is pretty grand. There are still many things I don't see as well as normally sighted people, yet I have managed pretty well.

I went to college and got a degree in photography and videography. I had my own portrait studio and also did fine art photography that I exhibited across the country. Then one day I thought, "Wouldn't it be great to help people with vision loss?" I never received many services as a kid, but I was grateful that my vision had improved. Now I wondered about those whose vision hadn't improved. Who helped them? I'd had the good fortune of having amazing parents and people who believed in me and helped me, so I wanted to support others and help them meet their goals and realize their dreams. I went back to school to get a master's degree in vision rehabilitation. Then, I worked at the Phillips Eye Institute for ten years.

I also earned my doctorate in health services with a specialization in vision loss secondary to a neurological incident. Subsequently, I came to Vision Loss Resources to work in the Community Services program. Five years later, I got promoted to president/CEO. Leading this organization enables me to encourage and support others in achieving their goals and fulfilling their dreams.

DAWN KULTALA
Niece Kelly Lynn

Kelly Lynn: my inspiration, my niece.
    She was born when I was a nursing student.

We learned she was blind.
    She would cry sometimes . . . bored in her crib.

She smiled.
    She didn't have to see those around her smiling
    to know how to smile; it was automatic.

We watched in awe and victory as Kelly took those
    first steps, unable to see.
    WOW, Kelly!

Braille, Beatles and Beatles (yes, I said Beatles).
Great conversationalist, very bright, and oh,
  so optimistic.

Kelly came home from high school, where they called
  her mademoiselle.
She calls herself the oldest cousin or the babysitter.
She has several younger cousins for whom she takes
  pride in setting an example.

PAC Mate, keyboard, dictionary, cane.
Kelly tells me that she is taking classes to use the
    iPhone.
My niece is by far more techno savvy than I, who
    can see.

Vision Loss Resources and mom are a great support.
I see Kelly and she puts a smile on my face.
She inspires me.
I adore her.

GARY BOETTCHER

Wrestling Blind

When I was eleven or twelve years old, I was told I was losing my sight. I lost 75 percent of my vision right away, but I could read large letters until I was sixteen. My fondest memory before vision loss was seeing scenery, especially farm pastures. I have Laurence-Moon syndrome—I can see light and dark in bright light. Otherwise, I can only see shadows.

I was extremely angry and bitter at first. I thought, "Why me?" I turned to alcohol for a while. At the School for the Blind in Grand Forks, North Dakota, I got sober. No alcohol was allowed, so if I wanted to stay at the school, I had to give it up.

When I first walked into the school, I was so nervous I almost fell over. My brother already attended the school, and my doctor confirmed it was the only option available. I had to make it work. A braille teacher was very patient with me and treated me like a regular person.

I attended a social studies class at the local junior high school. The principal had the wild idea that if I went out for wrestling, the other kids would get to know me. It would enable me to blend in. Pep rallies cheered me on. Shivers went up and down my spine as the spectators cheered and supported me.

After I finished school, my interest in sports continued. I took a self-defense class at Vision Loss Resources. I traveled with a beep baseball team. The ball beeps when it is hit. The team consists of a sighted pitcher and catcher, but everyone else is blindfolded.

Playing sports has taught me determination and helps keep my diabetes in check. Team spirit makes it fun.

My advice to people with vision loss is: Be patient; it's a huge adjustment. There will be frustration. But there are a lot of things you can do.

Can't? There is no "can't." You can still have a very rich, blessed life. Your attitude plays a huge role in what that life will be.

LINDA LEANGER

The Importance of Positive Influences in Our Lives

I am six years old. Waking up in the back seat of our car, the first thing that enters my mind is that I cannot see or hear our parents in the front seat ahead of us. I try to awaken my older brother who is lying beside me. "Nathan, wake up. Where are Mom and Dad?" There is no response. I shake him and try to awaken him again—still no answer. As I attempt to pull myself up against the seat in front of me, it collapses, and I slump back into my seat, falling against my left arm. I feel a sharp pain and then everything fades into blackness. Minutes later, I awaken again and see a man outside the car. My head feels so fuzzy that I don't know if he is really there or if I am imagining him. He sees me stirring and asks me my name. I answer, "Linda." He then asks me, "What's your last name, Honey?" I still remember he called me "Honey."

Later, I awake in the hospital, where Gladys, my mother's sister, stands over me. She is crying; I wonder why. She tells me her eyes hurt. I ask her why she doesn't tell the doctor. My doctor does not want anyone to tell me that my mother, father, and brother were all killed in a train/car collision. I am the sole survivor. I have a fractured skull, head concussion, broken arm and collar bone, and I am bleeding out of both ears. The doctors do not know for several days if I will make it or not. I keep slipping in and out of consciousness, and they do not have the equipment to determine the extent of my injuries. My aunt stays with me in the hospital and reads me many fairy tales to entertain me, as I must lie still. I love to sing, and patients in the hospital comment on how they love to hear my singing. When I am able to walk again, I pace back and forth in front of the window, looking for my parents' car, wondering when they will come to see me. The doctor fears I might go into shock if they tell me about the death of my family members, so I do not learn this until the day I leave the hospital. My cries of sorrow and grief echo through the corridors.

Now, after being released from the hospital, I am staying with my grandmother in my parents' house. There are too many painful memories of my missing family everywhere I look. Most of all I miss my older brother, Nathan. He was my friend, companion, playmate, teacher, and protector; I idolized him. He always looked out for his little sister. When we went up to his third-grade class to see a movie together, he would always save a spot for me on his seat. He made me feel secure.

Soon after I am released from the hospital, my grandmother sends me back to school, much too early. My teacher says to another girl, "Take this cry-baby to the washroom and wash her face." Does she not know that my life is shattered into pieces, and I don't know how to pick up the pieces and learn to live again?

Now, a couple of months later, I am living with my mother's sister and her husband. I feel much better here because it is familiar to me and I know them. I have stayed with them before. There are many animals on their farm, like soft, furry bunnies and kittens. I see cute newborn calves that struggle to their feet, fall down numerous times, then struggle upright again, finally managing to stand on stilted legs. Then they have to learn how to get their four legs to work together. Soon after I come to live with my aunt and uncle, they get me a little puppy. This puppy is so full of love that she knows how to take away some of my hurt.

Several months later, my uncle brings home a baby lamb whose mother has rejected him and refuses to take care of him. I can't imagine any mother not wanting this adorable creature. I am only too thrilled to be his mother. I feed him from a bottle. He follows me around like the lamb in "Mary Had a Little Lamb." I sing, "Linda has a little lamb." When he does not see me, he "baaas" in bewilderment, and when he sees me again, he leaps for joy; his legs jump straight up in the air as if they have springs in them. I am totally in love with this precious little lamb and would sleep in the barn with him, but my aunt and uncle draw the line there. These are such healing experiences for me.

During this time, I am aware that a big custody battle is going on, mostly for religious reasons, as some people want me to be raised in the same religion as my parents. I hear adults talking about where I might be placed. I hear them say that a family in California might want to take me. I do not know where California is, but I hear someone say that it is so far away. Then I hear another adult saying, "They don't take good care of their own children, let alone someone else's." This frightens me, as I don't know where I might end up—possibly with strangers? I sit on the floor, hugging myself and rocking back and forth while tears stream down my face. The pain inside me is so bad that I wonder if a heart can really break; mine feels like it could.

Finally, a judge takes me aside privately. I am sort of scared of him because of his long, dark robe. But he stoops down to my level and asks, "Linda, where do you want to live?" I tell him, "I want to live with Gladys and Gordon because I know them." This is where he places me. Later my aunt and uncle adopt me to ensure nobody else will take me away from them. I cannot call them "Mom" or "Dad." These words seem to get stuck in my throat, but this appears to be okay with them.

Several months later, I am back in a classroom

again. Another girl, who is like a little mother hen, befriends me and helps me adjust to school. She gets me interested in learning again.

At about age eight, I sing my first solo at church. My knees are knocking, my legs are wobbling, and I am shaking so much I fear people can see how nervous I am. But somehow I get through it. Teachers at school are impressed with my voice and ask me to sing in operettas like *Pinocchio*, as the Blue Fairy, and my adoptive mother makes me a beautiful frilly bonnet and matching blue dress to sing "In My Easter Bonnet" from *Easter Parade*. Gradually I acclimate to my new life.

Now, I am age twelve. I am in a study hall, and someone hands me my report card. Two Ds and a C minus? I shake my head in disbelief. Are they really there, or are my eyes deceiving me again? I squeeze my eyes shut and look again. Oh, no—they really are there! All of my grades have slipped. My eyes blur as tears fill them and stream down my cheeks. As I begin the long trek home, thoughts and questions flood my mind: "How had this happened? I certainly did not see this coming." Nobody had advised me that my grades were slipping. But I reflect back on the previous weeks and relive the times when the print on the pages faded and then blurred into a gray mist as I attempted to read my assignments. How many times did I have to close and rest my eyes for a minute before I tried again, only to have the same thing happen repeatedly? I have worked and struggled so hard. By the time I reach home, I am sobbing uncontrollably. This is totally unacceptable to me! As I enter the house, my adoptive mother asks what in the world is wrong. She cannot imagine what horrible thing has happened. I manage to sputter, "Look at my report card!"

Realizing that the problems with my eyes are affecting my schoolwork, my parents take me to an ophthalmologist. After the exhausting examination, the doctor tells me I have Stargardt's disease, a form of macular degeneration with juvenile onset, and am legally blind. He explains that I will need large print and tape recordings in order to do my schoolwork. He writes a note to take to my teachers, explaining that I will need special consideration during the long process of ordering large-print books and recordings.

When I present this note to a math teacher, he responds, "Well, as long as you are not trying to get by with anything." His words absolutely crush me. Haven't I always been conscientious about school? Already traumatized by what is happening to me, and not knowing the extent of vision loss ahead, his words devastate me.

My peers ask me questions like, "What's the matter with you? You going blind?" I have already begun asking myself the same frightening questions. I feel overwhelmed with the choices I will have to face in life: What about making it through school? College?

What about ever being a wife and mother? (Nobody ever played with dolls more than I did.) Will any man want someone with what I consider "missing parts"? And what about job choices? What will I be able to do? Will any employers give me a chance? My self-esteem is at a very low point. I determine that in my classes not only will I have to do well—I will have to excel.

Soon after my experience with the math teacher, my father tells me that another teacher said that he may have been a little hard on me, not realizing I was having so many problems with my eyes. "Why did he not talk to me?" I wonder. "Why go through my father?" I think how much more I would respect him if he had enough character to speak to me personally. Why do some teachers feel that by being apologetic to their students when apology is due, they would somehow lose our respect? Exactly the opposite is true. If he would have talked with me personally, my opinion of him would have grown six feet.

Given my past experiences with teachers, I conclude that they do not come automatically adorned with halos. Sometimes their tongues can slice sharper than any knife; they must earn my trust.

While in college, I speak to my English instructor ahead of time, explaining that I would need any tests blown up into large print or that I could take the test orally. On the day of the test I come prepared, but the instructor is not. She tells me that I am a "nuisance" to her, having to do extra work. I go back to my dorm and cry myself to sleep that night. But I rise with a new determination. I feel as if I am being punished for something that is totally out of my control. Sensing the injustice of it, I march to her office early the next morning, and I tell her that it is not my desire to be a "nuisance" to anyone, but that if I was going to make it through school, I would need extra help. I end my tirade by announcing to her that she needn't be bothered by me anymore; I was dropping her class and would pick it up with someone else. Later she attempts to apologize through one of my friends. Again, had she spoken to me personally, I would have had a lot more respect for her.

One day, while taking a timed test, I soon realize that the results of my test would not reflect an accurate indication of my abilities. I explain my situation to the instructor. He tells me that if I cannot take this test, I will never make it through school, and even if I do, I will never find a job. Again, I spend the evening in tears. But again, I rise with a new determination. I think, "Who does he think he is? God? He is trying to limit my life according to his measly expectations. I will show him what I can or cannot do." And I do! I not only make it through school with honorable grades, but in one of my classes over half of the students flunk out; I get straight As, and I find a good job, too.

These trials produced some characteristics in me that I may not have possessed otherwise, such as perseverance and stubborn determination. These traits have proved beneficial in many situations. But I have often wondered how many people in similar circumstances have been knocked down so many times that they were too defeated to get up and try, try again.

I thank God I also had some outstanding teachers, especially in the fields of music, speech, writing, and drama. They gave unselfishly of their time and energy, helping me achieve my goals. Most important, they showed confidence in my abilities and believed I could accomplish a lot. One example is a man who taught both band and choir in two schools. He took on projects far beyond what he was hired to do. He, at his own time and expense, drove me to Winnipeg, Canada, to meet a well-known voice teacher. He asked me to sing a solo part in a choral union that was composed of the best voices in the county. I was so thrilled to be a part of a full-voice, well-balanced choir—so much so that when the rest of the choir broke for lunch, I found a secluded place in the church and memorized all ten songs so I could enjoy the privilege and thrill of being a part of the whole concert. It tickled me when the director was quite shocked to hear me singing along on all of the songs, especially since I considered him the most ambitious and dedicated person I knew. He also spent time with me every week teaching voice and preparing me for vocal competition. He never expected less of me because of my vision loss; he expected me to do my very best. He arranged for me to audition for the Minnesota All State Choir. I was able to meet with other gifted students for a week of camp at Bemidji, and the final concert was here in the Twin Cities. It was one of the most thrilling experiences of my life.

Another amazing teacher directed choir in church, taught English literature at school, coached me in speech classes, and directed our class plays. Whenever I sought her opinion on something I was writing, speaking, or singing, she was always available and encouraging. That took real dedication and a sense that she was involved in something very important—the accomplishments of those she taught. I treasure the memories of these dedicated teachers and will forever be grateful for their influence in my life.

I have a lot of admiration and respect for the instructors at Vision Loss Resources, especially in the area of technology. Some of them have experienced loss of vision themselves, and they are competent, compassionate, and encouraging in their relationship with blind students.

How important it is that teachers realize what an awesome privilege and responsibility they have in shaping and molding future generations. They set examples that their students will never forget, either good or bad. Good teachers will inspire and encourage their students to achieve to the best of their potential; they must get to know them, their strengths, their weaknesses, and their needs. As I have experienced, teachers can make such a huge difference!

After going through many traumatic events in my own life, I believe the Lord has given me a heart of compassion and empathy for other suffering individuals. For the past twenty years, I have participated in the peer counseling program at Vision Loss Resources. We offer support and counseling to those who have recently gone through significant vision loss. We provide resources that can help them achieve and retain independence. Losing sight is truly one of the most difficult and devastating experiences, as it so greatly affects our functioning level in everything we do. As peer counselors, we interact with our clients, helping them to continue doing some of the things they enjoy, often by helping them find alternate methods. One of our objectives is to connect them with other blind/visually impaired people so they can learn from one another how to cope with vision loss and to solve some of their problems. There is great comfort in interacting with others with similar challenges. One of the many rewards and privileges for me has been to experience the joy of seeing people, who initially have been sobbing their hearts out, finally reach a time in their lives when tears are replaced with smiles and laughter. We cannot see smiles, but we can hear them. When a person is smiling or laughing, their throats are open, and their tone is much brighter and clearer. We learn to detect the emotional state of people by the different tones and inflections of their voices.

I also have enjoyed co-facilitating a low-vision support group, and it has been inspiring to see blind people interact with one another, sharing and learning the use of different devices and techniques to help them cope with blindness.

The community center has become a comfort zone for us, enabling us to meet and interact with others who are facing similar challenges. There are many choices of activities, so many that I tell others that if they can't find something they enjoy, they need to "get a life."

I have learned that through helping other blind people find enrichment in their lives, I have truly been the beneficiary of many blessings. I have been rewarded by meeting many amazing people who have, in turn, deeply enriched my life.

SUSAN ANDERSON

What I Learned When I Could Not See

The blindfold was put on and my world became dark.
I was told to make a grilled cheese sandwich.
    Ready, set, start.
I got tips and tricks on how to navigate the kitchen
    safely.
I buttered my bread, turned on the pan, learned
    when to flip.

The blindfold was put on and my world became dark.
I was told let's go for a walk. Ready, set, start.
I felt nervous, scared, and anxious.
I took each step with hesitation.
I thought I would trip, hit, or fall.
With my sense of direction I thought this was hopeless.
I crossed a street with a very loud heartbeat.
I made it in one piece,
    got lost in a driveway, but I found my way out.

The blindfold was put on and my world became dark.
I was told we were going to the woodshop. Ready,
   set, start.
I used a ruler to measure some wood,
used a power saw and planer with all my fingers still
   intact.

Amazing what you CAN do, when you put away the
   word CAN'T.
I learned that when the situation gets tough I can
   swim instead of sink.

DELORES FORD

Great-Grandmother with an Attitude: "I Can Do It!"

I am eighty-two years old. I grew up on a farm, and I first experienced vision loss in 1950. I lost my vision in a skating accident while playing hockey with my brothers when I was fifteen and had a concussion.

After I had surgery, I went back home, where I was one of eight children. My mother needed my help around the house, and she was the best counselor I ever had because I was made to do things in my own way. I finished my sophomore year of high school, then took a year off, and then went back and finished school.

I was twenty when I came to Minneapolis for vision rehab for three months. After that, the staff wanted to send me back home to my farm, but I didn't feel there was anything for me there. My sponsor helped me find a manufacturing job for about a year, and then I got married, became pregnant, and quit the job. Years before, my aunts and uncles had thought I shouldn't be doing some of the things I did on the farm. When I got pregnant, they worried again. People often think that blind people are unable to do anything, but I've always told people, "If it's possible to do it, I'm going to do it."

My husband and I are both blind. We worked in Business Enterprises, and we raised two children. I completely lost my vision at age thirty, at the same time I was diagnosed with cancer.

When I first came to Vision Loss Resources there was a set schedule of activities instead of personalized classes. I learned quilting from my daughter-in-law and began to teach the quilting class at Vision Loss Resources. I told students that the word *can't* was not allowed in my class. I told them about places like the store for the blind in St. Paul where I found a self-threading needle, which is very helpful not only for blind people but for sighted people as well. The store also has measuring tape, magnets, and books for the blind. I did most of my volunteering when I was middle-aged, after raising my children. I became part of the community service to help people learn how to do things in their own home. I was on the board of Vision Loss Resources for twelve years. I also gave talks to United Way and went to schools and visited with children about blindness.

Now I play cards, walk every week with the walking group, have fun, and take care of my house.

I have two sons, four grandchildren, and seven great-grandchildren.

Losing your vision at a younger age is much easier than losing your vision at an older age. I have tried to be a peer counselor and to keep telling people, "If it's possible to do it, I'm going to do it. There is always something out there you can do."

WALLY HINZ

The Typing Teacher

On March 30, 1977, I was up in Alexandria, Minnesota, on business. I'd gone out for dinner with prospective clients and decided that since I had business back in Minneapolis the next day, it would be better to drive home that night.

At about 11:30, I drove out of Alexandria toward Highway 52. It was snowing, and a blustery wind blew across the fields. I remember taking a left onto the entrance ramp but just then I hit a patch of ice and my car did a 360. Immediately I thought, "I've gotta find a place to turn around and get a room and call my wife." But as I continued to drive, it seemed as though the highway was manageable.

An hour and a half later, I fell asleep at the wheel, drove into the median and hit a tree. I was knocked unconscious. According to the highway patrol records, I lay there a couple of hours before they found me. I was taken to the hospital in St. Cloud. When I woke up that afternoon, I opened my eyes but only saw complete darkness. I didn't know where I was, and I didn't know what had happened to me. I was unaware that doctors had operated to repair internal bleeding, sutured extensive damage to my forehead, and identified compound skull fractures. I felt numb and disoriented. An ophthalmologist determined that the only chance I might have would be to go to the University of Minnesota for further surgery. The next thing I remember was riding in an ambulance with my wife, both of us scared to death.

A couple of days later I underwent right frontal surgery. A neurosurgeon confirmed the suspicion that the damage had been done and they were not able to change anything.

I stayed in the hospital for the entire month of April, including my thirty-fifth birthday, although I don't remember a second of it. What I will never forget is the exit interview with the neurosurgeon, Dr. Edward Selgeskog. He told me, "Wally, you're blind. The sooner you learn to accept that, the better off you'll be. Otherwise you'll waste all your time and the time of all of the people around you."

I didn't say anything in response. At that point, I wasn't processing information quickly because of the skull fractures. I thought to myself, "You're wrong, doc. I'm gonna get my sight back. Might take me six months, but I'm gonna get it back."

That was thirty-six years ago.

It took me nearly three years to understand, but that was the very best thing that he could have said to me. It was the pure, unadulterated truth. He did not give me any false hope. He made it clear to me what the starting point was for me on my journey back.

My wife and I were determined to handle the news.

I continued to believe I would be able to see; my feet were not on the ground. Neither of us had been exposed to blindness before, so how were we going to cope? I was assigned a counselor from State Services for the Blind, and it was decided that I'd come to Vision Loss Resources and take classes in order to adjust to blindness. At that time it was called the Minneapolis Society for the Blind.

On June 13, 1977, my wife and I walked through the front door of Vision Loss Resources. For seven months I took classes in braille, orientation and mobility, abacus, daily living, and typing, and every Wednesday afternoon I attended a Living with Blindness counseling session. All those classes were to enable me to hone my tactile skills, especially my sense of hearing in regard to orientation and mobility. They were designed for me to regain some confidence. The slowest skill for me to learn was braille. To this day, I've never become a rapid braille reader.

Things seemed to be going fine, but I had a sense that something was missing.

Nelda Daily Brown, an older woman, was my typing teacher. She was very serious about her subject and her students' progress. Nelda would dictate either a couple of words or a short phrase for us to type. I was always the last student to finish.

One day it turned out that I was the only student in class that period. I thought, "This is a great opportunity for me to show her that I've gotten better." But instead of dictating to me, Nelda sat down next to me.

"Wally, I'm not going to dictate to you today," she said. "I want to talk to you. There's something that you must always remember. And that is that you may be blind, but you are not handicapped.

"You have a lovely wife and a beautiful five-month-old daughter. God has given you talents. He's asking you to use them now. The journey back is not going to be easy. It's going to be a challenge. But you must always remember that even though you are blind, you are not handicapped."

And that's what was missing for me. True motivation. It was time for me to stop focusing solely on myself and the fact that there were so many things I couldn't do. The glass had been half empty, but it was time to take inventory. What did I have? What could I always count on?

All of a sudden I began to think in terms of the glass being half full. I had a wonderful wife and daughter. My wife had stood by me every day. It might have been an opportunity for her to think, "When we got married and I took those vows—for better or worse, richer or poorer, sickness and health—I didn't sign up for this," and yet that never occurred to her. Over the years she was unwilling to lower the bar of her expectations of me. She did not let me become a recluse.

Both Nelda and my wife played a very, very important role in my journey.

Today my daughter, Katie, is married, and I have a wonderful son-in-law and four wonderful grandchildren. Life is good.

VANESSA BONN

Have You Ever Stopped to Wonder?

Have you ever stopped to wonder how a blue sky
    can turn gray?
How the colors of the world seem to fade and melt
    away?

How the fear of noisy cars on the freeway going by
As you step across the street makes you wonder,
    "Why?"

Have you ever stopped to wonder how time seems
    to stand still
Or to peer into the future where the darkness gives
    a chill?

Have you ever stopped to wonder how it feels to grip
    so tight
Something long and white that helps you in the dark
    and in the light?

Have you ever stopped to wonder how it feels to
     listen most
When the loudness that surrounds you makes you
     shiver like a ghost?

Have you ever stopped to wonder how it feels to fly
     with ease
As you feel with feet and fingers that travel seems
     to set you free?

Have you ever seen your blessings and thanked Him
     for what you've got:
A sunrise, independence, and surroundings not
     forgot?

Have you ever thought of darkness, dreaming
     of black and a white cane?
Is there a future of no color or some promise
     or some pain?

Have you ever had the feeling of success that fills
     your soul
When you know the accomplishment of fulfilling
     every goal?

Have you ever faced the fear *and* the joy in your
     heart?
I HAVE!

MAUREEN PRANGHOFER

Seeing for Real

In the 1999 TV drama *First Sight*, a blind person falls in love. But that is not the end of the movie. Like so many other Hollywood depictions, life isn't really complete until the one who is blind becomes sighted. People have the mistaken notion that every blind person longs to be sighted, that once vision is restored everyone lives happily ever after.

I'm here to tell you that for me that was not the case. You see, I was not quite blind as a bat, but far from being sighted when a 1983 cataract surgery restored much of my vision.

Just like in the movies, I lay in a hospital bed, a bandage covering my good eye. The surgeon came in, removed the bandage, and I saw his hand! Did I cry, gasp, wonder, or exclaim out loud? No. I mostly looked around and noticed how awfully bright the world appeared. It was almost too bright. I wanted to squint, to back off from what was streaming into me. But, I knew from Hollywood that I was supposed to be breathlessly grateful and almost too excited and happy for words. So, I just said, "This is really cool."

I didn't know it at the time, but since that January day in 1983, I've learned why I was cynical, ungrateful, and not nearly as joy-filled as one might have thought I should be about regaining my vision. Nearly ten years earlier, I'd opened a door in my mind, a door titled self-pity. I'd gone camping to Yellowstone with a group of non-disabled counselors and disabled adults. We were a motley group, with some in wheelchairs, some with severe cerebral palsy, and one older woman who was born with the same physical disease I had. In addition to my blindness caused by premature birth, I'd also been born with a rare bone disease, osteogenesis imperfecta (OI). The disease causes bones to break easily. Consequently, my friend, Agnes, used a wheelchair and I walked with a long leg brace on my left leg. I'd never met anyone with my bone disease other than children at Shriners Hospital, where I'd spent several months as a child. So, it was awesome to be able to compare notes, to talk about the good and the bad, and to know that she understood the fears, the risks, and the constant unknowing of when the next break could occur.

But there was a hidden danger for people with OI there in beautiful Yellowstone Park. I noticed that whenever I walked somewhere, it was hard to breathe. I got easily winded and wondered what was going on. I soon realized it was the altitude. People with OI have varying degrees of respiratory problems, and though mine could be summarized in several bouts of pneumonia and one broken rib caused by sneezing, Agnes had much more trouble. In fact, she had so much distress that before the trip ended, she was flown back to Minneapolis, where she died within two weeks.

Her death caused that awful door of self-pity to open because I began having thoughts like "I am like her. I'm not going to live long." I told everyone, whether he or she wanted to listen or not, about my OI and about my vision problem. People became overwhelmed. They didn't know what to say or do. One time, while speaking with a personal trainer about how I could better exercise at a fitness center, he said, "I don't think there is any equipment you can safely use here." I became angry and disappointed. "Well," my husband said later. "What did you expect? You make it sound like you're made of glass." Made of glass? That wasn't the reality at all. Although I did walk with a brace and had some minor fractures, I was basically quite healthy. What I said and what I thought didn't match reality.

And here I was, after surgery, in a hospital room, where I didn't see things as they really were. In reality, I'd just been surgically given a fabulous gift. I saw well enough to watch TV for the first time. I could read using magnification glasses, and I could do my job much easier and could see objects as far away as half a block. But, I didn't see it that way. I saw the world as too bright, too busy, and confusing in a manner that made me wonder if I was going crazy.

Before I regained my sight, I'd decided what some objects looked like, what color they were. I'd made pictures of these things in my mind. For example, I recalled that when I was a small child, we had a thing to hold our milk carton that was bright yellow. So, in my mind that's how every milk carton holder had to be. But when I could clearly see color, I discovered that our milk carton holder was really olive green. You might say, so what? Who cares? But imagine doing that as you look at everything, finding out that what you had thought was not true. And, sometimes, I didn't know what things were at all. One time, for example, I was in the grocery store and saw some orange round things. "Orange and round," I thought. Oranges? No, they were big and piled on the floor. Well then, they must be basketballs. No. Why would they sell so many of those in a grocery store? So I went and touched one and immediately recognized the surface of a pumpkin.

Some things I could see, but some things I couldn't, and self-pity kept me looking on the downside of having my vision restored. Self-pity's objective is to eat up joy and every crumb of gratitude. It brings about self-loathing, guilt, and laziness.

During those ten years of having vision, I rarely questioned what I saw. I never learned to be joyful. I never learned to be thankful for the vision I had. I didn't see the beauty God had created around me; instead, I tended to focus on what was wrong.

And then as quickly as the vision came, it left. It vanished in a June 1993 accident in which I hit my head on cement and had what is similar to the shaken-baby syndrome. In four days, I became totally blind and ultimately had both eyes removed.

That accident was twenty years ago. Since then, through Jesus Christ, I've become more sighted than I ever was before. My self-pity is gone, and my life is filled with gratitude. I am thankful for the guide dog who now assists me. I am thankful for the wonder of technology that allows me to write using braille and a talking computer. But best of all, I've gained wisdom from knowing that true vision can only be obtained when one forever closes and locks the door of self-pity, and that seeing occurs when one can look beyond one's needs to see the needs of others.

PEGGY R. WOLFE

Two Streetcars and a White Cane = Braille

During the 1950s, my Uncle Matt had to give up his profession as a tax attorney in St. Paul because his vision loss from macular disease was so severe. He could no longer read. But, still in his early sixties, he was not about to give up.

He took two streetcars from St. Paul, with the aid of his white cane, and traveled to the Minneapolis Society for the Blind, the original Vision Loss Resources, where he learned braille. He sometimes took the streetcar to our house. In my early twenties, I was fascinated when he laid out his large braille sheets and said aloud the words his fingers were reading as they slid across the raised dots.

Though no longer able to work as a tax attorney, he became a volunteer at the Legal Aid Society, helping others for many years. A great loss for him was being unable to read books on the Civil War, so my husband-to-be and I visited him on Wednesday nights and took turns reading aloud his beloved books. I cherish the memory of those evenings.

Now, sixty years later, the gutsy example of Uncle Matt continues to inspire me as I enter my twelfth year of living with macular degeneration. Now I'm the one using the services of the renamed Minneapolis Society for the Blind!

FRANCES WHETSTONE
A Full Life

When the retinal eye doctor told me I was legally blind and there was nothing more that could be done, I felt like he had given me a death sentence. He should have said, "You can still lead a full life." But he didn't.

Yet God had a different plan for me. I found the right people and places to help me: the State Services for the Blind and Vision Loss Resources.

The best thing I ever did was sign up for a six-week Vision Loss Resources cooking class with Frank. There were six of us in the class and none of us knew each other, but by the time the six weeks had ended, we had bonded as if we had always been friends. I cannot ever thank Frank enough for all the help he gave me on preparing food, and all the tips he gave me on learning to live with vision loss.

Governor Mark Dayton chose me for a three-year term on the Rehabilitation Council for the Blind as a representative of the United Blind of Minnesota organization. As I was on the board of the organization, and we were always looking for new members, I asked if any of the cooking class members would like to join. They all did, and for many years we have enjoyed good food and fellowship together.

Many years ago I was a Bluebird and a Camp Fire leader. We sang this song to start our meetings: *Make new friends but keep the old / One is silver and the other gold.* I think back to this song because I have kept my old friends, but over the years I have made many new friends who are blind or vision impaired.

So sometimes if life hands you a bad experience, it may turn into a blessing, as it did for me. When I look back, I think I would never have known all these wonderful people and I would not have had the opportunities that I have had if I had not lost my eyesight. Now I am ninety-five years old, but I feel I have had a very full life. It was twenty-four years ago that the eye doctor said, "Frances, you are legally blind and nothing more can be done for you." Boy, was he mistaken.

ELLEN MORROW

Angels

"We all have angels guiding us . . . they look after us, they heal us, they touch us, they comfort us with warm, invisible hands."

— Sophy Burnham

My memory bank is full to overflowing from so many years of so many wonderful clients who have taught me and touched me in unimaginable, abundant ways. Yet one, I imagine, sits on my shoulder often, and she's always there when I need her most.

I met Kathy, a nun, early in my counseling career, when I was thirty-five. She came to us as a volunteer early in her vision loss. Among her many good works, she taught English as a second language. She was my age, had diabetes, and eventually contracted nearly all the complications that were so common many years ago. I am grateful they are not nearly so common today. Kathy's eyes, though her vision was fading, sparkled with enthusiasm and joy. She lit up the room at the group she facilitated with me. She managed the cantankerous, lecherous old guy; the angry ex–Hell's Angels member with his colorful explicative-littered vocabulary; the sweet artist who could no longer see her work; the isolated, lonely woman whose family and friends had abandoned her; and the two dear evangelistic gals for whom no burden was too great. She managed them and many others with love and understanding, but no pity! She said to all of them as her vision dimmed and her kidneys failed, "Our pain is such a rich teacher, if we can only but learn from it," and "Pain is the coin I use for Change."

After losing a leg, she revealed, "In order to move on, I had to sit naked in my wheelchair in front of a mirror, and give thanks for my body as it is." And move on she did, going to London to swim in the Special Olympics and learning to ski at Afton Alps. By word and deed, she inspired those far less disabled than she.

After her health declined, she moved to the convent's care center, where one day when I visited, the smell of donuts permeated the air. The scent evoked a memory of my grandmother, who made donuts; it was as if she was with me in the room! I shared my memory with Kathy, who explained that donuts were always made for funerals. For a long time after that day, Kathy would call me and say, "We had a funeral. Do you want a donut?" I did want a donut, but mostly I wanted to soak up her presence. Her physical strength faded, but her humor remained intact and her wisdom abounded.

For her final loving act, she learned how to play the

Celtic harp. "Nearly all the Celtic harp players were blind, Ellen," she mused with enthusiasm. She played for her sisters as they died, sweet music for their journey. She left us too early; I still had so much more to learn. Yet, she is with me still, sitting lightly on my shoulder when I need courage and inspiration, when comfort does not seem enough to offer others, when I don't know what to say. She reminds me of what I know deeply: the strength of the human spirit always prevails.

"We all have angels guiding us . . ." Indeed!

MARION FRIEDMAN
Life beyond Vision Loss

Over time, my eyesight began to change, and I became very concerned because I couldn't see well. I went to an ophthalmologist, who recommended that I undergo surgery. Each time I was scheduled to have surgery, it for some reason got canceled. Meanwhile, my vision continued to decline.

I decided to go to a new clinic, where I saw a young doctor, who immediately said, "You have macular degeneration, and you are going blind." Then, he turned and left. I felt appalled and shocked. I couldn't believe that he'd just walk out without offering me an explanation. I'd never heard of macular degeneration before, and I hadn't even dreamed that such a disease could happen to me. I thought: I'm going to be blind and dependent on everyone else in the world.

Two weeks later, I went to a seminar on macular degeneration. When the lecture ended, I went out into the hallway. Soon, a lady came up to me and said, "Hi, my name is Becky King." Becky started to talk with me about Vision Loss Resources. Then, she asked me how I felt about my vision loss.

"I am ready to cut loose and forget it," I said.

"No, no. You can't do that," she said.

Becky King gave me hope by telling me there were

things I could do, things that I could become involved in, and that I would have a full life. And, she said that I would not become completely blind. Still, when I went home I placed a bottle of pills by my bed.

Two days later, Becky King called me and asked if she could come to my home and check on me. During her visit, she gave me suggestions that helped me with everything. Then, two days later, Betsy McCartney, a Vision Loss Resources peer counselor, called and asked if she could help me. "Yes. Could you ever," I said. After our phone conversation, I decided there would be life after vision loss, so I put the pills back in the cupboard.

Betsy McCartney brought me back to life. If it had not been for her and Vision Loss Resources, I wouldn't be here today. Now, I'm productive and I feel worthwhile. I still have nightmares, though, about wanting to take those pills. Yet, that's behind me because I'm still here.

Based on what I've gained from Vision Loss Resources, I became part of the advocacy group, doing seminars for friends and families of people with vision problems, educating them on the different kinds of vision loss, and explaining how we can best help them. I've also given presentations in the community to groups with vision loss and have spoken at conventions for ophthalmologists and their staff who deal with people with vision loss. In addition, I've served as a peer counselor to about twenty individuals. I display my peer counselor certificate at home, with pride.

Time has gone by so quickly over the past twelve years. It seems as if I just turned around, and here I am at the wonderful age of ninety-two. Despite my vision problem, I've never had surgery, but I did have shots in one of my eyes. Now I have limited vision. Nonetheless, I'm proof that there is life beyond vision loss.

ROBERT ANDERSON

Letting Go

More and more, what I see just doesn't make sense to me. Yesterday I spent five minutes trying to decipher the most ordinary scene, one I see almost every day: the view from behind the bus driver. I sit there because I don't like tapping my white stick up a skinny aisle crammed with jutting knees, big feet, and wayward packages. It's a simple scene, compact and composed, tailor-made for my dwindling tunnel vision: the driver's back, part of the steering wheel, half of the windshield and its wiper, and just to the right, the fare box. But yesterday it was a jumble. It took me a full five minutes to unscramble and identify all the pieces before reassembling them into a coherent image, like figuring out one of those giant jigsaw puzzles.

As my retinas disintegrate, so does the world I see, fracturing into bits and pieces, and with every passing year, into smaller and more chaotic bits and pieces. Sometimes, in blacker moods, I wish my vision would go all at once, ending this messy business of going blind by slow degrees. But I never wish that for long. I cling like crazy to every last scrap and shard.

I often wear a cap with a visor, which I previously used to cock high or low as the light demanded, to keep the glare of the sun or a lamp from wiping out my fragile field of vision. I'd make sure I sat or stood facing away from bright lights so I could see the features of the person I was talking to, or I'd ask them to move under the light so I could see them better. When I was looking at something, I'd shade the sides of my eyes with my hands like blinders, or cup them into a pair of makeshift binoculars to constrict the light and sharpen the image. I was adept at continually shifting from regular glasses to sunglasses to no glasses at all in a juggling act designed to maximize my ever-dwindling scraps of vision. I had a bag full of tricks, but I've grown tired of them, tired of the tedious routine of trying to extract, like a desperate alchemist, ever more stingy drops of golden light from a world turning rapidly to the dross of dull lead. I've grown tired of the constant effort and attention.

This entire process of going blind, starting with night blindness in adolescence and progressing till all that remains in middle age is a keyhole of clear vision in my right eye, has been a subtle negotiation of limits and possibilities. If I give up too soon, I give up too much; if I hold on too long, refuse to relinquish what I cannot keep, fight too stubbornly against the inevitable, I risk rage, bitterness, exhaustion, and despair. There is a time to fight, and a time to let go. What is the middle way?

Lately I've begun to explore giving up the struggle of trying to make sense of what I see and relaxing into not seeing, accepting confusion and trusting in what my other senses and intuition tell me. I've discovered there's an ease, a serenity in letting go.

The choice crystallized for me recently as I stood in the back of the formal garden in the St. Paul Conservatory listening to a guitarist play some Irish ballads for St. Patrick's Day. I stopped trying to make sense of the crazy-quilt of mothers and kids and babies and old folks and flowers and trees and shrubs spread out on the terraces before me—a motley made all the more puzzling by the shifting light that played through the great glass-domed ceiling above, dappling the scene below.

I recalled the effect this space had on me as a child, when I could see it whole and intact. It was a stately garden under glass, its long terraces and promenades lined with rows of ornamental cypress and yew and banked with the blooms of the season, that descended tier upon tier to the narrow reflecting pool below. There, to my childish eyes, lucky pennies glinted in the sunlight like the floors of heaven.

I remembered what this room looked like thirty years before, when I came to sketch its foliage for my freshman art class. My tunnel vision was still generous enough for me to navigate without using a white cane, and it sharpened my focus and attention to detail as I peered into the intimate anatomy of an orchid. To me, this had always been a wondrous and magical room.

There was a time, and not too long ago, when remembering all this beauty and being able to see only generic shapes, fragments, and inchoate flux, nothing that evoked any claim on my imagination, would have driven me almost wild with despair. But this time I did not hang on to what I once possessed; I did not chafe at my loss. I let go. I leaned back against the wall, pitched my cap high, took off my sunglasses and let the warmth of the noonday sun flood down luxuriously upon my upturned face. I melted into the scene, its sounds and smells, its dappling of colors, its glints and shadows, as effortlessly as losing myself in a painting by Monet.

Originally published in *Turtle Quarterly*.

LOUIE McGEE

Blindness—It's Not as Simple as Black or Light

My name is Louie McGee. I am twelve years old, and I am blind. Not the kind of blind you think about when you hear the word *blind*, but blind according to my doctors. Well, blindness isn't as simple as black or light. I have a rare eye disease of the retina called Stargardt that takes away my central vision. And that's the strange thing—losing *part* of my vision.

When I was five years old and heard that I had this disease, the idea was hard to understand. My parents seemed worried, and everyone was careful to say "visual impairment" rather than "blindness" when they talked about it. I always figured being blind meant that all I could see was black, and that wasn't how it was for me. I had this disease, but it didn't hurt and I could still see the same stuff I was used to seeing. I played with friends the same as always. I woke up in the morning and checked to see if my vision had changed, but I could still see the morning light. I could still see my sister Carmella's face when she was standing there asking me if I was awake.

After a couple of months, my mom, dad, sister,

grandma and grandpa, and I went down to Iowa City to see a new eye doctor. I spent an entire day in the clinic there. Everyone was really nice, but the tests were crazy. Hooking up electrodes to my eyes. Sticking my head in a bowl. Looking at little dots. Giving some of my blood for testing. At the end of the day, doctors spread my eyelids wide open to take pictures of my retinas. Dr. Ed Stone told us he thought I had Stargardt.

Every year we repeat this trip to Iowa City to spend a day with Dr. Stone looking into my eyes, testing things, and taking blood and pictures. I don't get treatment or medicine because there isn't anything anybody can do for this. There is no cure. I go to the doctor to find out how much more of my vision is gone. It's strange, but as you live with this each day, you can't actually tell. You need a doctor to keep track of it all.

Sometime after that first visit to Iowa City, my mom and dad found the Foundation for Fighting Blindness, an organization focused on developing a cure for blindness. That's right—figuring out something that will stop this disease and allow me to see again. It's really like that stuff you read in the Bible. First I thought it was crazy that nobody had already figured out any treatments or cures for blindness. Then I was surprised that a group of people was raising money for doctors and researchers to figure this all out.

When we discovered the Foundation, it was organizing the first-ever VisionWalk in Minnesota. My mom and dad signed us up, and we organized "Team

Louie." My mom and dad, my sister Carmella, and many family and friends joined strangers walking around Lake Harriet to raise awareness and money to come up with a cure for me and the millions of others with eye diseases.

That same fall, I went to kindergarten. I remember my mom and dad talking a lot about which school would be best for me. They chose Highland Catholic School in Saint Paul. When I started there, I already knew a couple of kids in my class. Although I had a vision teacher and a mobility specialist, I didn't feel I was different than the other kids and they didn't treat me differently.

That Christmas Mom and Dad asked Carmella and me where we wanted to go on vacation if we could go anywhere. They seemed a little obsessed with making sure I could see some cool stuff while my eyes were still good. Well, we said we'd love to go to Hawaii. And just like that, Mom and Dad were figuring out how we could all go. That March, they pulled me from school and Carmella from preschool and we hopped on a plane for Maui. We saw a volcano, a tropical rain forest, and whales. We went to a coral reef in a submarine. I thought if that was what blindness was going to mean to me—bring it on. I didn't have too much trouble seeing any of it.

The following fall in first grade I noticed things started to get a little bit harder. We were all learning to read. For me, the words were getting smaller and I really couldn't make them out very easily. If I turned my head away from the book, I could sort of read with the sides of my eyes. This seemed to work okay, but I decided I wouldn't raise my hand to read out loud. My mom and dad came into my class and explained to the kids about my eyes. I don't think anyone really understood what it was like to have partial vision. People seem to understand needing glasses and total blindness, but this in-between stuff is harder to figure out.

By third grade, I got this great big magnifying TV called a CCTV to help me read. I was seated right by the door because my CCTV needed an outlet and there weren't many outlets in my classroom. That meant people could walk by and see me and my CCTV and then they knew I had something wrong with me. Sure, it was cool for the boys to look at warts and scabs close up, but did I really need this? Then it got worse. In fourth grade, I was given a white cane. No way was I going to use that. I could see well enough to ski, run track, and play soccer, and my balance was pretty good so I could stay up when I tripped. My parents told me just to learn how to use the cane and we'd deal with this as it comes. As far as I could tell, it was all coming a bit too fast.

In fifth and sixth grades, I was asked to be the Youth Chair for the Foundation Fighting Blindness VisionWalk. I made some good adult friends at the Foundation, Julie and Mark, who helped me learn to talk about my disease and the research to cure it.

It seems like each month over the past year I have heard about a new clinical trial that is curing one of the diseases those of us with some level of blindness face. My friends at the Foundation Fighting Blindness even nominated me for a national community spirit award for volunteerism. There were 28,000 people nominated; one hundred were chosen to go to Washington, D.C., and then the top ten youth volunteers were selected from that. I was chosen as one of the top ten youth volunteers for 2013! My mom and dad came with me to Washington. I met kids my age from every state and heard about the stuff they were doing, helping people in their own communities and really making a difference in the world.

This year I also had an opportunity to join six others with Stargardt disease to lead a panel discussion at Vision Loss Resources in Minneapolis. I was the only kid. We all talked about how this crazy disease probably leads us to be better people: better students, better workers, better athletes. Imagine that, something like blindness actually making people better at something. As we talked, a guy in the front row, with some sort of blindness himself, blurted out, "That's a load of crap." He was an older guy who clearly wasn't happy with his situation. Truth is, none of us are happy that we have this, but that was the first time I faced someone who was just plain mad about it. That day I learned a hard lesson, one I hadn't really faced before. There are two roads to take: one of anger and one of hope. Black or light. While I'm starting to understand black, I choose light.

At the beginning of this summer I got a message from my friend Julie about a guy with Stargardt who is involved in a clinical trial paid for by the Foundation Fighting Blindness. His vision sounded just like mine. After a single (experimental) treatment, he could see again. He didn't just get better partial vision, his blindness was actually cured—cured by research supported by the work Julie, Mark, I, my family, and all the volunteers and staff at the Foundation are doing every day. Actually my friends Julie and Mark aren't just volunteers, they are super-volunteers. They both have an eye disease and are successful adults. They are great role models and have helped me understand that the hope I have is real, something we can all believe in, share, and continue to work toward.

As I look ahead, I am entering seventh grade full of hope. I love playing soccer, skiing, running track, and being on the swim team and will continue with those sports. As I write this story, I'm out on Isle Royale in Lake Superior with my family. We have been hiking and searching for moose. I have a lot of great friends and mentors and imagine a bright future. I am certain we will find a cure for this disease. Even if we don't and I continue to lose more of my vision, I know I will do more great things. After all, blindness isn't as simple as black or light.

PEGGY R. WOLFE

Why Did It Take Me So Long?

After a few years living with macular degeneration, I asked my retinologist if there might be a support group for people with vision loss. He suggested I call Ellen Morrow at Vision Loss Resources, but I didn't follow up on his suggestion then. I kept the idea of calling Ellen pretty well buried in the back of my mind until my retinologist brought it up again during subsequent visits. Still, however, I did nothing.

When I finally made the call, it had been four years since the doctor first told me about Ellen. By then, it had been eight years since my initial diagnosis. Kate Grathwol conducted my initial interview and enrolled me as a client of Vision Loss Resources. At my first meeting with Ellen as my counselor, I kept hearing peals of laughter from the next room. I was invited to join the group of men and women having a wonderful time eating the lunch Frank Alden had prepared in a demonstration. All the people in this group had severe vision loss.

I was seated next to two women who are members of Vision Loss Resources' advocacy group and involved in community education. They go to various facilities and tell groups about the services offered by the center. The women had also received training to become aides to assist staff members who moderate support groups. These inspiring women showed me how much someone with severe vision loss could contribute, even when living with peripheral vision only.

Enrolling as a client at the center changed my life. My resolve to keep a positive outlook was affirmed and bolstered by meetings with Ellen. Other staff members have guided me in various ways as well. I have met amazing people in classes and at the many functions at the center. In Frank's weekly life skills class, I learned new ways to live, including special cooking techniques, how-to ideas for the all-important organization skills I needed, and an upbeat approach to dealing with the frustrations of living with vision loss.

Why did I wait so long to take the first step in seeking help? Ellen said it was because I was not ready earlier. She told me that people come to the center at all stages in their disease; there is not a single "right" time for everyone. The right time is when one is ready. Sometimes I wish I had been ready earlier, but I think a streak of stubbornness got in my way.

JOHN LEE CLARK

I Didn't Marry Annie Sullivan

My wife and I often encounter the usual assumption many people have about a couple like us. She is Annie Sullivan to my Helen Keller. In their imaginations, I am always with my wife. I cannot take a single step without her guiding arm. She is my link to the world.

We know this is the picture in their heads because of what they say. People would approach my wife to say she is a saint. People would tell me that I'm so lucky to have a wife to cook for me, clean for me, and drive for me. Now, my wife is the most wonderful person I know. I'm indeed lucky. One glimpse of her personality from when we first met at Gallaudet University: She was telling her girlfriends about her new boyfriend, and they wanted to know who he was. She told them that surely they'd seen this tall, handsome, brown-haired boy from Krug Hall. They weren't sure. As she tried to help them place me by sharing more details, one of them asked her, "Do you mean that deaf-blind guy?" "Yes!" "Oh! Why didn't you say so?" "I forgot."

The truth is that I do half of the cooking for our family of five. Also, I am a neatness fanatic—for me, cleaning is like breathing. The men in my family have never been strangers in the kitchen, and they don't consider it unmanly to kneel and scrub the floor. I have simply followed their example, and being deaf-blind is no reason not to.

And what about driving? Yes, my wife drives the car when we pile in. But she rarely ever drives for me. It's only when our family is going out together or the two of us are on a date. When it's a board meeting I need to attend or a presentation I'm giving or a literary event to meet up with some of my writer friends—things that are for me and not for her or our boys—I take care of my own transportation.

Sometimes my "driving" myself places takes the form of a city bus, a paratransit van, or a taxicab. More often, though, I employ an accessibility assistant, who picks me up and gives me all sorts of visual information as I do my errands. Sometimes, even when it's an event that my family is attending together, I have my assistant there so I can participate fully without having my wife think or process things for two.

It has long been my policy, whenever we relocate and are looking for a place to live, to ask myself, "If I lived here alone, would I be all right? Would I be independent and be able to get around, shop, and socialize in my community?" If the answer is no—because there is no transportation access or there are no deaf-blind services—then we need to look elsewhere. My asking that question doesn't mean I'm ignoring the essence of marriage, family, or community, which is interdependence. No one is truly independent. However, there is such a thing as unhealthy dependence.

Unfortunately, some deaf-blind people are stuck in situations where their dependence on partners or family members puts them at risk. Society should be responsible for ensuring that we have the same resources, rights, and accommodations that hearing and sighted people enjoy, but this doesn't always happen. This can complicate the lives of deaf-blind people, including their relationships with others, especially significant others.

I was blessed to have many deaf-blind guides in the matter of marriage and interdependence. One was Robert J. Smithdas, who wrote in his first memoir about becoming engaged to a hearing-sighted woman. Many of his friends praised her and told him that she was perfect for him—she was generous, attentive, and so helpful! Bob wanted to get married, badly, but he had mixed emotions. As the wedding date approached, he realized that the relationship was wrong. He dropped the engagement. He wasn't able to fully articulate why, but after reading his book, I understood. He wanted a wife, not a helper. He wanted to be a husband, not a charity case.

Bob would later fall in love with a deaf-blind woman whom he had met for the first time by literally bumping into her. Talk about love at first contact! But when they tied the knot, the media unfairly made them into a "Believe It or Not!" exhibition—even National Enquirer ran the story. Few appreciated how sensible and normal the pairing was: most people, after all, do marry others with the same culture and background.

Another role model was Harry C. Anderson, the former president of the American Association of the Deaf-Blind. He and his deaf-sighted wife, Elaine, stayed at our home when I was a teenager. They were in town for a retreat of families with deaf-blind children. Harry gave a training session on interdependence and used his and Elaine's life together as the model. He showed us that, while there were things he couldn't easily do, he and Elaine were able to divide all of the daily chores and responsibilities equally between them. That made a simple but lasting impression on me.

Even with such positive models, my wife and I had to learn many things by trial and error. For example, some people would tell her to tell me hello. At first, she would relay their messages to me. Soon, though, we sensed that this was not a good idea, and she began to tell them to come over and say hello themselves. Also, I have had to say "No" a lot when people assume that, because I have a sighted wife at my disposal, I could go somewhere at the last minute, read something in an inaccessible format, or take a videophone call. I gently but firmly steer them toward working with me by adapting to my needs.

Not that I never borrow my wife's eyes. I do. It's usually for quick fixes, not unlike her borrowing my height to reach something on a high shelf or borrowing my hands to open a jar. The point isn't to avoid helping each other or supporting each other. She tenderly nurses me when I'm sick, and it's my shoulder she turns to when she weeps. The point is to be aware of how society has placed me, as a deaf-blind person, at a great disadvantage in some situations, and to correct these problems in the right away—not by having my wife take on the burden and be the solution, but by confronting these barriers and tracing them back to where the real solutions are. My wife is a brilliant and assertive partner in that endeavor, as she is in all our other endeavors, and that's why I'm a very, very lucky man.

AMY SUMMER

Vision Loss and Vision Found

As I approached the counter to place my order at the juice bar, that all-too-familiar feeling came over me. The menu board hovered above, taunting me like a carrot on a stick—almost within range of my vision, yet just out of focus. I could make out key words like *strawberry* and *banana*, but as far as figuring out the price and size for my smoothie, let alone the choices for an optional booster ingredient—I was left to my own devices. "How much is a large smoothie?" I asked, thinking I could skate by without having to reveal my struggle with my compromised vision to the total stranger waiting for my order. "The price is right there, ma'am," he said curtly, waving his hand toward the menu board, as if I was an alien or had just emerged from a cave. I felt my head, neck, and shoulders clench. My go-to "Get around the Vision Problem" plan had been foiled, and I heard myself saying, "I know, but you see I'm a little bit vision impaired."

My counselor at Vision Loss Resources has reminded me on more than one occasion that I live in both the sighted world and the vision-impaired world. Situations like struggling to read signage and overhead menu boards are an everyday occurrence for me. At work, I need to enlarge the font for material on my computer so I can read it more comfortably. Even though my Kindle and my iPad help me to increase the size of the print for the books and newspapers I love to read, I still make sure I carry a small magnifier with me for when I need to double-check a receipt or the price of an item on a restaurant menu. When I am among other vision-impaired and blind people, how-ever, I admit to having a mixed bag of feelings: guilt mixed with gratitude about my compromised vision. Vision Loss Resources has helped me to reconcile and merge those feelings so that I can understand, accept, and embrace my unique vision story.

My ophthalmologist could diagnose the retina problem in my left eye and manage the glaucoma in my right eye, but he couldn't treat the panic and anxiety attacks that happened after he said I would need surgery to remove a cataract in my right eye. Un-fortunately, most doctors (ophthalmologists included) don't have the toolkit to treat the emotional aspects of vision loss. All I could think of was losing my re-maining usable vision, even though I was reassured that cataract surgery was a slam dunk and that eye doctors practically did them in their sleep. Fortunately for me, I had heard of that building at the corner of Lyndale and Franklin in Minneapolis that has—for al-most one hundred years now—been assisting blind and vision-impaired clients like myself on their own personal journey of vision loss and vision found.

A MOM

Societal Progress

We visited our family in Ely, Minnesota, around the year 2000. My daughter must have been about eighteen years old. My aunts, mom, daughter, and I gathered at a delightful little restaurant, the Northwoods, to enjoy a meal together. While we decided what to eat, my daughter, who is blind, politely listened to me read the menu to her so she could select her meal. One of my aunts observed this lengthy process, while the waitress kept coming back to see if we were ready to order.

Mind you, a sighted person can quickly scan a menu to find an item. But, if the menu is not in braille, it's impossible for a blind person to read it. Therefore, someone must read the menu to a person who is blind until he or she hears something that sounds delicious. Eventually, we ordered and enjoyed our meal and each other's company.

Some time after our trip to Ely, my daughter received a package in the mail from my aunt. She had sent a braille menu from the Northwoods restaurant, a gift card for a meal, and a warm-hearted note, explaining that she wanted to be sure that when her great niece visited Ely again, she would have the ability to read the menu and order her meal. My aunt's gift to my daughter filled my eyes with tears of joy. Not only had I advocated for my daughter, but also one of my aunts really understood what it meant to have the ability to do something that seems to be a simple, daily thing. She offered this gift at a time when very few if any restaurants, even those in the Twin Cities, had a braille menu.

Her gesture reminded me that we don't always know who will pay attention to certain details or when. For my aunt to take the initiative to get the menu transcribed into braille involved so much effort: recognizing my daughter's need, taking the time to obtain the copyright permission from the restaurant, researching how to get the menu transcribed, and contacting the State Services for the Blind to have it done. Think of the effort and expense, and finally the delightful surprise sent to my daughter!

Years later, we started to find braille menus in some large chain restaurants in the Twin Cities. How refreshing! Now, we have the luxury of the Internet, where many restaurants offer their menus online, enabling one to read the menu prior to visiting the restaurant.

But, this is possible to do only if one has the technology to access the Internet, the equipment to search with screen-reading capabilities, and the braille display to read the braille menu. Or, one can have the menu read via screen reading, though it is cumbersome since web pages aren't always user friendly to screen-reading software. Moreover, not all people who are blind have access to technology that enables them to gain access to online menus.

My story about my daughter living with blindness in everyday life may seem unique. But Vision Loss Resources provides blind individuals with the opportunity to live independent lives by offering classes and services, and holding events in the community. Vision Loss Resources creates a symbiotic relationship between the individual and society to affect a positive chain of progress for all people.

KELLY

Shopping Preferences for Blind People Like Me

I live in a managed home. Every other Monday we go shopping at Walmart. I don't like the way one of my housemates thinks about me: she thinks that if I don't want to learn about different soaps, my mom should take me shopping. She thinks that I should be coaxed into knowing what is in the store, what the prices are, and all of that. My housemate doesn't like to leave me out of listing everything on the shelf, but I don't *like* learning what's on the shelf. I can't smell shampoo, I can't smell lotion, and I can't smell lipstick or lip gloss. She likes to browse in Walmart, Target, Kmart, and the grocery stores. And malls. This particular housemate would like to waste time in *any* mall. She is always excited to tell me about shampoo and soaps and lotion. Because she is enthusiastic about looking at every shelf, she gives me a synopsis of the entire store. How do I tell her that she doesn't need to? Instead of the staff advocating and supporting me, this person wants to describe everything. I like to just grab what I need, pay, and walk out.

My mom doesn't explain what's on every shelf; she just picks up whatever she needs and moves on.

Just like me. When she buys my soaps and shampoo, I don't go with her, because, like I said, I can't smell shampoo. She buys shampoo and bar soap that aren't expensive, in order to save me money.

The noise in Walmart is loud because of the fan. Plus, I don't like talking to that annoying greeter. He stands by the door to greet people and always asks me about the staff that used to accompany me. But recently this man tried to know my business. I would rather he didn't try to start conversations with me or ask me questions about other people. One time after he bothered me, he turned his attention to the staff that was with me. "What's your name?" The week after that, he asked, "Give me a letter," "Give me two letters," as he wanted to guess the letters in her name, and on and on. Finally the lead staff person stopped him from asking me questions that I don't want to answer.

If the staff goes into any of those stores with me, it helps if they ask, "Kelly, do you want to put your earplugs in?" I use my Walkman in the store, but my mom thinks I'm a fruitcake because of that. Actually, when I go into the store, I automatically put my earplugs in. When I go for a walk, I use a Walkman. It helps me to focus on where I'm walking instead of on the conversations in the store. Really, I would prefer to order from the Internet and have things delivered.

KELLY

Just a Few Hints

Being blind is perplexing, but along with it comes
   bumps that are enriching.
A bit of orientation and mobility makes you feel
   uncomfortable
But in the end, leaves you in tranquility.
The bumps are the braille, enchanted like a tale.
Tools like braillers and slate and stylus keep you
   writing.
Feeling braille with fingertips is like seeing with
   your eyes.
When searching for things misplaced by others,
   haste makes waste.
Respect and trust are a must.
Just because there is no sight, doesn't mean that
   I'm not bright.
Your goals and my goals are not all going to be the
   same, but also not different.
Being blind is not a shame.
You may think I'm strange, but I'm not; I'm normal.
Just because I'm blind, doesn't mean I have to be
   confined.
My relatives, my aunts and uncles lift up my mind:
They want me just the way I am.

CORALMAE "COKE" STENSTROM

Life-Changing Experiences

L ife changed for me in the fall of 2000 when I moved to a house next door to my family in New Brighton, Minnesota, after living for forty-two years in my home in Park Ridge, Illinois. I had recently been told I was legally blind and would be facing lessening vision with age-related macular degeneration. My daughter had attended a seminar at the Earle Brown Center and learned through the doctors of the University of Minnesota about many eye diseases. There were vendors there that day, and she signed me up for information from Vision Loss Resources.

Shortly after moving to New Brighton, Jerry, a Native American staff member from Vision Loss Resources, visited me in my home and informed me of what was available for people with low vision. It felt wonderful to be right next door to family after struggling the last few years in Illinois with lessening vision. More changes started to occur about a year later when I attended an in-service at our church and listened to Julie from Vision Loss Resources staff about vision loss and possibilities of help. One of the things she mentioned that day was the possibility of having a peer counselor, a person who was visually impaired, be available by phone to answer my questions and help me adjust to a new way of life. Things really started to change when Sister Gabriel became my peer counselor. She encouraged me to sign up with Metro Mobility and not feel like I should rely solely on my family for transportation.

In late fall of 2001, I started the use of the Metro Mobility bus and went to visit Sister Gabriel at her convent for a luncheon on the last day of the year. It was helpful to talk with her, both in person and over the phone. In the spring of 2002, I was invited by Vision Loss Resources to take the bus and go to classes in order to become a peer counselor to help others with low vision. Once a week for fourteen weeks I went to class with a book, lectures, and assignments, having family members read me the information at home. The classes opened my eyes to what was available and gave me the chance to meet lots of interesting people with wonderful stories to share. Each month, peer counseling included a community speaker and education for all of us to expand our understanding of the many types of vision loss and what services we peer counselors could tell others about to encourage them. Dodie was instrumental as volunteer coordinator, keeping peer counseling vital with client referrals, teaching us to document our work, and planning an advocacy group that was open to all. That vitality has continued ever since, with a monthly meeting at which clients make contact with lots of new people. Soon I was encouraged to become a member of the peer advocacy group, and there were monthly meetings to discuss how best to get out the word to people about Vision Loss Resources. One of the first advocacy projects was to get safer signal lights at the intersection where Vision Loss Resources is located.

SUZANNE PAULUK

The Society for the Blind/ Vision Loss Resources: Then and Now

The summer of 1971 was the beginning of my adult life, a time to prepare for college and learn to live independently. Looking back, it was the most memorable summer of my life. I was part of a summer program called the "Project" for blind students who had graduated from high school and were preparing to go on to college, vocational school, or jobs. During the day we had classes at the Society for the Blind. We lived in one of the classic old mansions that had become sorority and fraternity houses near the University of Minnesota campus.

I had skills that not all of the students going to the Society had. Since my mom had started teaching me to cook in my freshman year of high school, I was a pretty good cook by that summer, and I enjoyed trying new recipes at the Society. As a landlady of housing for University of Minnesota students, my mom was always surprised when students moved in never having learned to make their beds. She made sure I knew how to do that long before I was ready to move out of the house.

There were other important skills I needed to learn in order to be independent and do well in school. I learned Braille 3, which is similar to shorthand, and how to use an abacus to do basic math. This sounds old-fashioned now, but I still use an abacus to count rows in knitting, since row counters are not accessible without vision. Mobility and cane travel were also very important. I must have presented a real challenge for my instructor, because I have a terrible sense of direction.

One of the especially important things I experienced that summer was living with a peer group. During grade school I had been on a routed cab ride with other blind students, and was with blind students at school. However, since we were from all over Minneapolis we could not get together after school to play or do homework together. Later I went to my local high school, where I was the only blind student. Living with other blind students in a dormitory setting, taking classes together, and participating in recreational activities gave me the experience of "just hanging around" for a whole summer.

Our sorority was within walking distance of Dinkytown, a vibrant community located on the north side of the University of Minnesota campus. The heart of Dinkytown is a four-block area filled with restaurants, bookstores, and unique small shops that at the time carried everything from clothes to incense, candles, posters, and other decorative items that were popular with college students in the early 1970s. The area surrounding Dinkytown housed students, artists, and people living bohemian lifestyles. There was and still is a neighborhood of people of eastern European heritage who had moved to the area during or soon after World War II. We loved living in this area because we had such a diverse choice of shopping and restaurants. In that atmosphere, we shared the hopes and dreams of what we could all do and be.

We were given an allowance for eating out and paying for other expenses, with some spending money left over. Since it is very hard for blind students to get jobs, this was the first experience most of us had with our own money to budget. For some people, eating out was a new experience. Going to restaurants was another opportunity to practice skills we were learning. One of our favorite restaurants was Vescio's Italian. Once we had chosen the restaurant, we got directions and used our mobility skills to get there. Often the servers had never served blind people and did not know how to interact with blind customers. We needed to ask them to read the menu and the bill to us, and we learned how to be assertive in a positive way.

We often thought that we taught the business and restaurant staff more than we learned. Back then, people had less interaction with blind people than they do now. Often people would speak loudly and slowly, believing that because we couldn't see we also could not hear them. One evening when we were walking to a restaurant, someone asked us how we had all known, at the same time without saying a word, that it was safe to cross the street. We explained that we listened to the direction of traffic in order to determine when it was safe to cross. The "Project" helped us to integrate the skills we learned at the Society for the Blind into our adult lives while we had some adult supervision.

The next fall I went to the University of Minnesota, Morris. I majored in English and minored in Spanish and spent one summer in Mexico. I was married in 1974 to Roger Pauluk. My husband and I have worked with people with physical and mental disabilities in several ministry positions, and I have written the newsletter for our current ministry, Care & Share, since 2004. I also have worked for several companies over the years, including the North Hennepin Human Service Council, where I worked with service providers for people with physical disabilities and/or mental retardation. I have been a customer service/claims representative and have provided services for many programs, including Sun Country Airlines, fraud and identity protection, and entertainment and travel coupons and discounts, among others. I am currently working for a company that evaluates websites for accessibility using my screen-reading and magnification software.

Although my husband has spina bifida, we owned a camper and enjoyed camping for several years. I have always loved to read and go to concerts and theater productions. I used to have a pretty big vegetable garden, and during that time I froze and canned produce. I still enjoy cooking.

Now, after forty years, I am again benefitting from the services at Vision Loss Resources, for recreation and health. I enjoy participating in the walking group, where I have lost some weight, renewed old friendships, and made new friends. I was especially excited to find out that Vision Loss Resources had a knitting group. I had not knitted for over thirty years because I had no one who could teach me how to pick up stitches and advance in my skills. Being part of the Vision Loss Resources knitting and crocheting group is a lot of fun. We make and donate baby afghans, lapghans, chemo caps, comfort shawls, booties, and hats to charitable organizations. Now I can also help others with knitting and crocheting. It feels good to share, and being a volunteer helps me maintain a positive attitude when I am going through hard times. Having benefitted from volunteers who have helped me, I know how much I appreciate volunteers and how rewarding volunteering can be. I feel better knowing that if I lose more vision or hearing, or am left alone through the death of my husband, Vision Loss Resources will be there to help me find new ways to do things. I know that volunteers are available to shop with me, read my mail, and set up online bill paying. Knowing that Vision Loss Resources is here for my current and future needs is very reassuring.

Thank you, Vision Loss Resources, for being there for me throughout my adult life. I hope Vision Loss Resources will be around for the next hundred years.

JULIETTE SILVERS

My Claim to Fame

So I went to the bank, across the street from my job at the New York State Department of Employment. When I approached the teller to make a withdrawal, he asked if I had not made one earlier in the day. He then informed me there was nothing to withdraw. I was shocked; obviously I hadn't been in the bank that day. Usually, a very friendly bank guard assisted me as well as some blind customers who worked in the Department of Social Services. Charlie had taken the day off.

I informed the teller that I wasn't leaving until I got my $2,700 back. He responded that this was impossible because the bank was closing shortly, at 3 p.m. I then marched to the Department of Social Services to inform the blind people employed there to be on the lookout. They couldn't believe what had happened to me. I went home and called the FBI, as well as all the city newspapers, telling them of my plight.

The next day, at 10 a.m., the FBI and TV stations with cameras were at the Bowery Savings Bank en masse. Bank officials told them that cameras were not allowed. "Where were you when my money was being ripped off?" I responded to the bank officials.

It turned out that unbeknownst to me, the guard

"handling" my account and those of other blind customers had been helping himself to our cash while reporting our deposits and withdrawals to us as if no theft had occurred. The guard claimed he needed the money to purchase a wheelchair for his son. The bank claimed he had been an excellent employee up to that point. He was arrested, and I'm not sure how his life went after that.

That night, the president of the bank came to my office and returned all my money. This incident happened in 1970, and from that point on, blind people have been required to go up to the tellers and do their transactions themselves. Articles were written about this incident in newspapers; a stranger even sent me a braille copy of one of the articles. Years later, someone came over to me on the subway and asked if I was the woman whose money had been stolen.

More than this type of notoriety, I like to tell people that I'm better known for having gone to high school with Barbra Streisand and that they can see her picture in my yearbook.

LYN JOHNSON

That Fellow with the Bucket of Yellow Paint

His handiwork can be seen in the painting of the public access areas at government buildings, medical clinics, strip malls, big-box stores, and more.

I am talking about the fellow responsible for the painting of curbs, pedestrian walkways, and handicap ramps at each site.

Being a very creative guy, he treats each public access area as a blank canvas. This creativity is subject, however, to varying degrees of inspiration, since he does a more thorough job at some venues than at others.

For example, at one big-box supermarket, he painted a nonexistent curb (actually a flat area) yellow and marked it "NO PARKING." He also painted the pedestrian walkway with diagonal yellow stripes. For the handicap ramp, he painted the entire ramp yellow and stenciled the handicap icon on it in blue and white. There is no established color at the local, state, or federal level. Law says you have to have the ramps, but there is no guidance on color choice. That's the trouble.

At another big-box supermarket less than a block

away, he painted the curb yellow, the pedestrian walk-way with yellow diagonal stripes and left the handicap ramp unpainted. Apparently he ran out of inspiration, or paint, or both.

A few miles away, at the public library, he painted the curbs yellow, but completely ignored the handi-cap ramps, which, in places, take up about two-thirds of the width of the sidewalk leading to the library's front door. The pedestrians need to be careful when navigating these slanting areas of sidewalk, espe-cially in icy and snowy weather.

At the strip mall, he painted the curbs yellow and stenciled the handicap icon on the ramps—this time in yellow instead of blue and white.

He must have been tired by the time he got to the local restaurant. There he painted the curbs yellow and added the outline of a box, in yellow, on the hand-icap ramp. Then he painted a large yellow "X" inside the box—I guess to mark the spot?!

Going from one venue to the next, he remembers to paint the curbs yellow but has difficulty remem-bering the color scheme he painted on the previous handicap ramp.

I really would like to have a talk with that fellow with the bucket of yellow paint. We need to discuss the merits of being creative versus those of being consistent and uniform—especially as they relate to painting handicap ramps.

The problem is, that fellow with the bucket of

yellow paint is very elusive. I'll have to find him first, before we can have that talk. Maybe then he will understand how frustrating it is to be visually impaired and how often the visually impaired depend on the colors of curbs, walkways, and handicap ramps to offer the right information.

JENNIFER DUBBIN

White Cane Mutiny

It was the end of my first week in rehab at Vision Loss Resources. Various emotions were going through me, especially anger. "Why do I have to go through this?" "What did I do to deserve this?" "I don't need this training." I have spent most of my life denying I had a visual impairment. I thought of myself as just like every other kid.

That morning before my mobility lesson, I met with Ellen, my counselor. I was having trouble expressing my anger at the situation, but pent-up energy coursed through me. As Ellen and I talked, I looked down at my cane. I thought to myself, "If only I could take my anger out on my cane." A lot of my anger and shame stemmed from the white cane.

I got up enough courage to ask Ellen if I could break my cane. Understanding how I felt, she gave me permission. Immediately, without further thought, I took the cane and broke it over my knee. I felt my anger drain from my body and into the cane I had just mutilated. I had rid myself of that problem for the time being; however, there was a new problem. I had my mobility lesson next period and didn't have a cane.

I was beaming from ear to ear, but how could I justify my actions to my instructor?

Fortunately, Ellen accompanied me to my mobility instructor's office to explain what had happened. I stood in the doorway of her office, wondering what she was thinking as she saw the broken cane in my hand. When we explained the situation to her, she was very understanding. But, she told me, I couldn't do that again. It was funny for just this one time. We all laughed.

I had taken out my intense emotions on an inanimate object, and I felt relieved. Not every counselor will let you crack a cane over your knee. Since that time, an artistic 3-D picture of a cane being cracked over someone's knee has been posted at Vision Loss Resources. It is reassuring to know that I'm not the only one to feel this way about my cane.

NIKI MATTSON

Minneapolis Mobility Mania

I am no stranger to orientation and mobility (also known as O & M) lessons. As a child, I had to learn to get around new schools, and the high school seemed overwhelmingly huge to me. I also took O & M lessons every Monday afternoon at the Burnsville Center when I was fifteen or sixteen. I am from the suburb of Eagan, and although Eagan is now a city all its own, it was a hick town when I was growing up, with dirt roads and only one or two small malls and shopping centers. So I was not used to "Big City Life," but I sure got used to it fast!

The other day my mother commented, "I don't know how you found your way around that mall. I still get lost!" And I replied, "Well, they've changed a lot of things since 1989, Mom." But now that I think about it, I don't know how I did it either. Those mall maps were hard to read even with perfect eyesight, and I used a magnifier. Actually, I think I was lucky. Had I been born any later, the O & M instructor might have had me navigate the Mall of America!

For two summers in the late '90s, I participated in a program called Summer Work Evaluation Program.

Every weekday morning during the three weeks, our group had to find its way to the center for vocational training. This meant hopping at least one city bus. But I wasn't on my own, and I, along with the other "newbies," just followed along. Once I forgot some papers I needed and didn't realize it until I reached the dorm at St. Thomas University where we were staying. At first i was scared about traveling by myself. But I found my way back to the center and returned to the dorm and was quite pleased with myself for not getting lost.

I entered Vision Loss Resources in the mid-1990s, and along with learning how to cook and other everyday tasks, I needed to learn more mobility skills. Unfortunately, my mind fails me as to who my instructor was, but I think her name was Mary. At first, she had me find places in the neighborhood, especially since I would probably be moving into one of the apartments that Vision Loss Resources provided at the Bryant Towers building up the street. I needed to find the grocery store, Burch Pharmacy, and so on. After a few weeks of success, Mary had me taking the bus.

First I had to call the place she wanted me to find, ask their address and the easiest way to get there from where I was, and ask how to find the nearest bus stop. Then I had to call the bus company, ask them about times, which bus I needed to take from point A to point B and/or C, and how to get back. This was before the Internet, Google Maps, and GPS.

The first few bus trips were not very difficult—just a few blocks or a mile farther than I had already walked. Then they got trickier.

I am very shy, and asking a bus driver "Can you tell me when we get there, please?" was a *big* step for me! But I bit my lip and pushed myself. Most of the bus drivers obliged when they saw the white cane. If it was a busy time of day, passengers would give up their seat for me, which I find is still true today. Not everybody in the city is an ax murderer!

Mary would follow behind my bus in her car, or if it was a short distance, on foot. One day I was feeling very confident, so I didn't ask the driver to tell me when to get off. Poor Mary! When she didn't see me get off, she zoomed up behind the bus at the next stop and pulled me off. "Why didn't you get off?" she asked me. I could hear the worry in her voice. After that happened two more times, she said, "You better ask the driver every time you get on that bus, because I'm not Mario Andretti; I can't always catch up to you!"

Although I thought it was funny at the time, I was relieved.

Eventually I rented an apartment at the Bryant Tower building and got to know Minneapolis very well. There were times when I didn't take Mary's sage advice and just hopped any old bus and wound up across the city where I definitely didn't want to be! That was before cell phones, so a few times, I had to hitchhike back home. I did meet interesting people that way; in fact, that's how I met a lady who belonged to a church group. She got me interested in her group. After attending their group for a few months and getting to know the other members, I was baptized.

Of course, I do not suggest hitching—especially nowadays. Even in a town like Eagan, anything can happen. I've learned not to be so shy, especially if I don't want to end up across town. I still take buses from time to time and haven't had horrid experiences, except for a guy who stalked me, but that's a different story. Now, of course, if I have to go farther than five to ten miles, I call Metro Mobility—that's what they're there for!

MARY NICKLAWSKE
Orientation and Mobility Specialist

The Invisible Observer

After working for twenty-five years in the field of orientation and mobility, I have racked up some great stories about my clients: their dedication, determination, bravery, mishaps, and weather adventures! However, I wanted to write something that tells more than just a story about me or a client. I think my clients would appreciate a story that gives readers that Oprah "aha!" moment to think about and see themselves from a blind person's perspective.

Orientation and mobility specialists have unique views of a blind person's day out on the streets of town. Many times we work as a silent observer during a client's mobility lesson, just watching from a few steps behind, ready to help if needed but wanting to let our client be as independent as possible as he or she navigates a situation such as walking to the store or boarding a bus. To the average person walking down the sidewalk, mobility specialists are another fellow pedestrian sharing the sidewalk or simply an invisible observer. This invisibility gives us a wonderful opportunity to watch how people react and respond to the white cane or guide dog user. Often my clients don't even know what had transpired until we are finished with our lesson and I tell them. *You know that door you couldn't find the handle to? Well, there was someone standing there holding the door but he didn't tell you he was holding the door, so you had to keep looking for the handle!* Why don't people just say something like "Hey, I am holding the door open for you"? It seems simple, I know, but a lot of people seem to think a blind person can suddenly see them standing there with the door open. Maybe people think a blind person can somehow *feel* it? Or maybe people simply aren't thinking at all, like those who ask me if I know sign language when I tell them I teach folks who are blind and visually impaired. Hmm. Think about that one.

I am not trying to make fun of anyone here. When I point these things out to people, they usually can laugh at themselves and appreciate the advice on "what to do when you meet a blind person."

I find it especially interesting to watch as a blind person approaches a group of people who are talking on the sidewalk. One of the people in the group usually spots the person with a cane walking toward them and alerts the others. It fascinates me that, as soon as people see the person coming at them with a cane, they freeze and stop talking! So now there is a group of people standing in the middle of the sidewalk *not* talking. If they continue to talk, my client can hear them and attempt either to go around them or to say "Excuse me," and wait for them to move apart. However, when the people standing there are quietly staring, my client has no chance to go around because he or she doesn't know they are there! Instead the group starts to jump out of the way with shocked smiles on their faces like a bunch of frogs diving for the water, panicked that "Oh my gosh, that person is going to run into me!" Please, everyone, if someone is coming at you with a cane, either keep talking, move aside, or say something so the person knows to go around you.

Now let's talk about appropriate touching. Do you know how pregnant women complain about complete strangers coming up and patting their baby bump? Well, every cane traveler out there has a story or two or one hundred about being pulled, pushed, grabbed, and carried places he or she had no intention of going. One day as I was following a client, a man came up to the intersection where she was standing, did not say a word, grabbed her cane tip, and started pulling her out into the crosswalk. My client had no idea what was happening. She thought maybe a dog or a cat was pulling on the end of her cane! She let go of the cane and stayed in place. The man was completely perplexed as to why she wouldn't come along with him and even went so far as to yell at me for not helping her. "I have been watching you! Why didn't *you* help her?" Here's why I didn't help: not every blind person standing at the corner needs help! Sometimes a person is listening to traffic to determine if he's lined up to cross properly. Sometimes she is waiting for a bus. Sometimes blind people are waiting for the light to change, and sometimes they are just hanging out. The appropriate thing to do is to say, "Hi! Do you need any help?" No touching, pushing, grabbing, or carrying is necessary.

Saying hello is a great thing to do: it's friendly and polite. However, picture putting on a blindfold and walking around your office, school, or neighborhood. Now everyone who walks by you is going to say, "Hi Bob! Do you know who this is?" Will you recognize that voice? Will you recognize every voice that says hello to you? Most likely you won't, and you will feel very bad when you have to ask, "I'm sorry, who is this?" This happens all the times to my clients! Everyone knows him or her as the one blind person in the school, office, or neighborhood. If my client sees you when and where you're expected, most likely he or she will recognize your voice and say your name. But blind people don't always recognize your voice, and they'll feel terrible that they can't place it. Think about how bad you feel when you can't remember someone's name! Please say your name *every time*. "Hi Bob. This is Mary." Bob will let you know if you don't need to say that, but until then, keep saying it!

We all do the best we can with what we know. And most of the time, people really are just trying to be friendly or help out. My hope is that after reading these few short examples, you will think a little bit more the next time you see someone with a white cane and know what to do or say.

DIANE O'SHAUGHNESSY

Get Ready, Get Set, Go!

As a near-blind person, living alone, I spend a lot of time talking to myself, and to pets, and to inanimate objects, especially when I am stressed out or feeling rushed. Today is one of those days.

Come on, fingers, work with me.
You have to feel what I can't see.

I must get ready, can't be late.
Oh, why did I procrastinate?

Mirror, Mirror on the wall,
I can't see me in you at all.

Is my head too small? Is my hair too big?
I'll trust in you, my handy wig.

Now for you, makeup. Where did you go?
I just put you here ten seconds ago.

Aha! There you are. Now let's get to work.
Mascara first, and try not to jerk.

Dark pencil for liner; light pencil for brows.
Got them mixed up, but I don't know how.

These should go on without a hitch.
If only I knew which one is which.

Good morning, kitties, so furry and plush.
Which one of you girls ran off with my blush?

Oh, there you are, all pink and pretty.
Oops! I brushed some on the kitty.

I almost forgot. I need to get dressed.
My closet just feels like such a mess.

Black clothes on the left; white clothes on the right.
I finally gave up the color fight.

Only in my wildest dreams
would I know what colors are in between.

So black pants it is, and a creamy white sweater.
Or, maybe it's pink, or tan, or heather.

Brusha brushabrusha, my trusty Oral-B.
With luck, I finally found you . . . in the kitchen pantry.

Ring, ring! My doorbell! The "big bus" is here!
I'm packing you up—my purse, cane, and gear.

Riding the Metro, I'm now on my way
to a brand-new adventure, an exciting new day.

JEFF MIHELICH

My Camping Trip

This past August I joined others from Vision Loss Resources' community center services on a camping trip to the Apostle Islands on Lake Superior. The trip was a joint effort between Vision Loss Resources and Wilderness Inquiry, also known as WI. When we were on the road to the Apostle Islands, I was more than a bit apprehensive. I'm not a camping kind of guy. My notion of camping is not having cable TV and not having a king-size bed. But I wanted to try something new. I thought, and it was true, that doing this with others who are blind or have low vision and staff who know how to assist us would be the safest way to give this a try.

We stayed in tents on property that WI owns very close to Lake Superior. It was about a five-hour trip for us, so the first day was spent traveling and setting up camp. We checked out the kayaks and the canoes we would use. We were given a wet suit and provided with a sleeping bag and/or sleeping pads if we did not have them. I'm so glad we did not have to put up the tents. WI keeps this campsite up for the summer so the tents don't come down at the end of the weekend. Since the tents are set up on platforms, they are not directly on the ground. I was happy for this during the night when we had a very bad storm. The sound of the rain hitting the tent made it seem like more rain than it actually was. In the morning, the ground was damp, but did not look like what we had feared when we were listening to that storm.

WI requires that all participants wear a wet suit when in a kayak or canoe. We also had to practice how to get out of a kayak if it capsized. We had to dress up in our wet suits, a life jacket, and then a poncho that covered the opening of the kayak after we climbed in. The kayaks were tandem, so two of us took it into the water. WI staff walked us out a bit, then instructed us on how to safely get away from the kayak when we flipped over.

I will say, it was very strange trying to flip over a kayak; it was something that you would want to avoid, not something you would want to do. But in any case, it was my turn. We flipped the kayak, and I think I drank half of the lake by the time I made it out of the water.

WI prepared the meals, with some of us assisting. WI has it down to such a science that it was sometimes faster just to stay out of their way and let them handle it. WI was more than impressed at the number of pots of coffee we drank in the morning. Cowboy coffee, boiled just like my great-grandfather did. No power at the campsite—so people crashed early, around 10:30 p.m. I thought it was closer to midnight myself . . . all the good fresh air, I guess.

The next day we took one canoe and three kayaks and went around a bit of a marsh that feeds into the lake. It reminded me of the Everglades—tall cattails and weeds and a narrow path of water for the canoe.

I have to fast-forward and tell you about the last day. We took one canoe and three kayaks along the shore of Lake Superior to the cliffs that have caves cut into them by the wave action from the lake. That part of the lake is made of sandstone, not at all like the north shore we have on this side. Because it is sandstone, over time the wave action broke down the stone and made caves. We were able to take our canoes and kayaks *into* some of the caves. It was so amazing—you could just feel the age of your surroundings. I could touch the wall and see how it crumbled under my touch. I could see horizontal lines of colors in the rock face, differing hardness and composition of the rock that resulted in the colored layers.

Looking back on it, I was very proud of myself. I took some risks by trying something that I would not normally do. Walking around in rough, uneven terrain was not my idea of fun. But it turned out that it *was* fun. And it helped make me more confident to take walks along the paved walkways we have around the lakes here at home.

NANCY FRITZAM

Weaving Baskets and Friendships

It's Tuesday late afternoon, time for our basket weaving class with Frank. We have our assigned seats with tubs of water before us. For three years, I've been weaving, soaking, packing, snipping, and tucking, not to mention twining, shaping, shaving, and putting on the rim. Each basket is a work of art. I pick a color, choose the style, and then pray it turns out beautiful. Fortunately, Frank is a master craftsman. Just when you think the basket has no shape, he shrinks, bends, and packs it in such that all of a sudden the basket's form is perfect, and you can't wait to finish it.

Our time together isn't only about basket weaving. We gather to discuss great books, recipes, and life's little ups and downs. The baskets I have made while sharing with others become gifts for Christmas, weddings, birthdays, and showers. To make crafts and visit with friends is a wonderful thing.

KATI GALLAGHER
Programs Assistant, Vision Loss Resources

Vision Loss Resources, A Culture of Kindness

In one way or another, I have always been involved in work that focused on serving others. So, when I was laid off from a position I had held for many years, I looked long and hard for a job where I could again engage my heart as well as my head. When I researched the Vision Loss Resources' website, I saw their mission, values, and a comprehensive list of services that convinced me I might find a home there.

I began working at Vision Loss Resources in August 2013. I had often driven past this building, but I didn't know what a gem of an organization was thriving behind these walls! A "culture of kindness" is high on my job wish list. I have found it here at Vision Loss Resources.

Clients arrive with the seemingly impossible task of regaining their independence and getting back into the work force while living with vision loss. After several weeks of instruction in orientation and mobility, technology, and other areas of training, they begin to understand that more is possible than they ever imagined. The Rehabilitation Services instructors do outstanding work by guiding their students with a tried and tested blend of current techniques, up-to-date information, patience, and encouragement. I feel fortunate to be associated with such an incredible team of dedicated and skilled people.

LORI MCCLURE

A Love Affair
with the Twins

For the successful completion of a course in fire prevention, the fifth graders at Wenonah School won or received tickets to a Minnesota Twins game. On a hot, sunny day in July 1965, I went to my first Twins game. When I entered Metropolitan Stadium, the home of the Twins, I thought it was the most beautiful place I had ever seen. The outdoor stadium was very colorful, and so were the people inside. The smell of popcorn and hot dogs hung in the air. The cheering crowds and the crack of the bat are sounds I will never forget.

In September 1965, the Twins won the American League pennant and were headed to the World Series! My fifth-grade teacher worked for the Twins during the summer. He was a baseball fanatic and wanted to involve his students in his love for the game. He made watching the play-off games a real learning experience. We learned how to keep score and calculate batting averages.

We also researched the history of baseball. For me, that was the start of a lifelong interest in the sport.

During the mid-1960s to the early '70s, I played

softball with other girls from my local park board. Once, while I was at the park, I met the daughter of Minnesota Twins player Jimmie Hall. She took me to meet her dad, and I got his autograph. In high school, it was my dream to marry a professional athlete. Even though that dream never came true, I never stopped loving the game.

Years later, when I married and raised two daughters, I shared my love for baseball with them by taking them to several games. But now, due to a degenerative eye disease, it became impossible for me to see the game being played. So, the radio became my new best friend. Even though I no longer could see the play-by-play action on television, the sights from the ballpark remained vivid in my imagination. I remained a loyal fan throughout my life, the highlights being the Twins winning the 1987 and 1991 World Series over the St. Louis Cardinals and the Atlanta Braves.

Early one morning in October 2003, I called WCCO radio to participate in a contest. Someone was going to walk away with two tickets to an American League play-off game. At the time, I was a rehabilitation client at Vision Loss Resources, taking courses in adjustment to blindness. When I arrived later that morning, I said to my orientation and mobility instructor, "Guess what? Instead of my scheduled lesson, I need to go to WCCO studio and pick up the Twins tickets I won."

While walking down Seventh Street in downtown Minneapolis, I encountered a roped-off area in front of a hotel. A gentleman came out, guided me around the obstacle, and I continued on my way. After picking up the tickets, I returned via the same route. This time, however, not only was the obstacle still there, but so was a large crowd of people. Once again, the same gentleman came out of the hotel, and this time he told me what was going on. He said, "The New York Yankees are exiting the hotel and boarding their bus to head for practice at the Metrodome." Having the tickets in my backpack, I was thinking how nice it would be if I could get a Yankee player's autograph. Had I known at the time that the Twins were going to lose the game, I would have plowed through the crowd and tripped the Yankees starting pitcher with my cane.

I attended that game with my mom. The atmosphere of a play-off game is like that of no other. Even though I could no longer see the action on the field, the sounds and smells brought back fond memories. The boys of summer will forever be imprinted on my mind's eye.

JESS CRELLY
My Story

For someone who has near-perfect vision and no need to even wear glasses, working with someone who was blind was intimidating, even a little scary. Up until my third year of college, my only experience with someone with low vision was with someone who was aging. Then, a man in his fifties spoke in one of my classes, and at the end of his presentation he shared about his wife's recent blindness and asked the group for help. Something made me jump at the opportunity. I am not sure if it was the emotional story he told or the fact that he had almost given up.

The first meeting with this man and his wife—I will call her Sue—gave me butterflies in my stomach. I was scared, worried if I knew enough to be able to help her, and feared I would mess up. Once I met Sue, I was compelled to simply listen to her, her story, her experiences, and what she needed. While listening, I realized that our communication was vital to her health. Sue was starved of the opportunity to speak to anyone other than her husband and doctors. She was looking for someone who would listen and talk with her.

I thought when I started I would visit a few times

and then be done, but I was hooked after the second time we met. I loved working with Sue: she taught me things, and I taught her things. When I asked her what her goals were and what she wanted to get out of our time together, her answer was simple. Sue wanted to feel whole again, and for her that meant communicating with other people, shopping, and getting back into the kitchen.

Over the next sixth months, I worked with Sue once a week for a few hours each time. We started working together in September, and within a few months she was set to go. Most of Sue's accomplishments came when she gained confidence that she could do the things she wanted to do, only in a different way.

At our second meeting, Sue wanted in the worst way to make cookies for her granddaughter's bake sale. I went and found a recipe for cookies that did not need to be cooked. The recipe was simple, but the process seemed very daunting to Sue. We went through it step by step, and by the end of it we were both covered in chocolate and felt proud of what we had accomplished.

Other times we memorized the layout of the grocery store, prepared pies for Thanksgiving, and got her email up and running, but most of all I was there to listen and share easy tips and tricks to making life easier for her. Once, I went through her cupboards laying down outlines in tape for what item should be on which shelf so her husband would put things back in the right place. It was all the simple changes that made life easier for Sue. Another simple thing I suggested was to have her wear a baseball cap in the kitchen so she would not hit her face on her cupboard doors.

Sue taught me that life is wonderful, that even the biggest challenge if broken down into steps can be accomplished, and that blindness is something that happens. It changes the way we do things but should never dictate how we live our lives.

GARY HENTGES

Using Binoculars When You're Blind

In 2002, when I became legally blind, Valerie from Vision Loss Resources would come to my home to give me tips and techniques for coping with everyday situations. Part of the training was using a set of binoculars because I had trouble identifying street signs.

I'd go out each day and practice with the binoculars so I could pinpoint where street markings were. One day Valerie accompanied me as we walked about two and a half blocks from my house. I stopped at an intersection and tried to focus the binoculars on the other side of the street so I could read the street sign.

I must have been standing there for five or ten minutes when two Brooklyn Park police officers showed up. It suddenly dawned on me that the people inside the house across the street had noticed me looking in their direction and must have thought that I was a Peeping Tom! Valerie and I explained what I was doing, and I don't think I'd ever heard police officers laugh so hard.

When the officers went to the house to explain, my neighbors also laughed. But it reminded me of how innocent things taken for granted can be misinterpreted.

Another incident happened at a shopping center. I was peering in stores to try to figure out where different aisles were marked, and as I was going from store to store, I'd stop at each entrance to try to see which store it was. I was trying to get to Sears, when lo and behold, I stopped at Victoria's Secret and almost went in!

These innocent mistakes can happen to those of us with low vision. It makes us realize at times we need to laugh at ourselves and yet learn from the mistakes.

JERRY KLOSS

My Story

I received my cane mobility from Vision Loss Resources way back in 1973, when their old entrance was along Lyndale Avenue, before the remodel of the building.

Tom Langham was my instructor, and I still remember the day in my advanced class when he said, "If you can take the bus to the restaurant at Lake Street and Lyndale in the southeast corner, I'll buy you breakfast."

This was the beginning of a new confidence for me, as I was able to collect that free breakfast. What a special moment. *I can live with blindness*, I felt.

My story also includes a horrific moment that turned positive. At that time I had about fifteen years of employment on the books at MnDOT's Golden Valley office when, unannounced, Tom showed up at my desk with the white cane. I was horrified. All I could think about was, "Here goes my employment."

Many of my fellow employees knew I had sight issues, but I kept it under the rug as best I could.

Tom had me walking the halls, moving through doorways, and so on, and my best assessment was, "Well, I guess the whole world knows now."

The bright side of all this was yet to come. Fellow workers greeted me by name, stating, "I did not know you couldn't see me when we passed. I just thought you were not too friendly."

These are just two highlights of what I would call "adjusting to blindness in the workplace."

PEGGY R. WOLFE

The Befuddled Servers

On the final evening of my visit with my daughter in Iowa City, we had dinner at our favorite restaurant. Since it was a lovely August evening, we decided to sit at an outdoor table. We planned to splurge on the tenderloin steak, salad, and vegetable. There were two servers, elegant in their long black aprons. I asked that my steak be cut in the kitchen, because it was difficult for me due to my poor vision. I was quite proud of this bit of self-advocacy. I knew I wouldn't have to spend time struggling to cut my steak and then give up and hand my plate over for my daughter to help me.

Soon the two servers arrived and set our plates before us. Dusk was falling by then, but I could see that the large, dark hunk on the far side of my plate had not been cut per my request.

In a disappointed voice tinged with scorn, I exclaimed, "But I asked that my steak be cut in the kitchen!"

The two servers looked at each other with bewildered faces, and then looked at my daughter for help.

She said, "Mom, that's your salad!"

I burst out laughing, followed by my daughter, and then by the two servers, who were relieved to know how to react. I was pleased when they joined in our laughter.

The situation defused, we all enjoyed the hilarity of my mistake. This evening is now one of my fondest memories.

LYN JOHNSON

A Second-Generation Friendship

My friend just called and said that she is running late again. Her job as a bank teller requires that she balance out before leaving for the day. It doesn't really matter because we still will have plenty of time to do some grocery shopping and run a few errands. My devoted friend has helped me every Saturday afternoon for the last five years. The story of our friendship goes back a long time.

In 1960, my family had just moved to the Como Park area of Saint Paul from Frogtown. I was seven and getting ready to start third grade at a new school. My nineteen-year-old sister had just secured a job as a sales clerk at the G. C. Murphy Company in Midway Center. One day my sister came home and told us that she had met a new employee, a high school student named Ginny Houseman who was working there as part of an on-the-job training program.

A few days later we went to the store and met Ginny. During our conversation, my mother found out that she and Ginny's mother, Velma, had been very good friends during their high school years.

At home my mother showed us a snapshot of her

holding my four-year-old sister's hand and Velma holding the hand of her three-year-old daughter Mary while carrying a six-month-old Ginny. It was the only photo of Ginny's family in the album.

In June my sister attended Ginny's graduation open house. Gradually, their friendship faded.

Fast-forward to 1980 and my first day working as a tax accountant at 3M. Ginny Morgan stopped by my desk and asked if I wanted to go to lunch.

Ginny and I hit it off from the very beginning. We both liked to sing, so we joined the 3M Women's Chorus together. We spent many hours rehearsing and laughing about wrong notes and bad harmonies. When we sang at our first Christmas performance, our families met. It was then that we discovered that Ginny Morgan's maiden name was Ginny Houseman.

When I left 3M after fifteen years, Ginny and I still got together on our respective birthdays and at the holidays.

Then, in 2008, my vision started to fade and I was no longer able to drive.

Well, Ginny just now pulled in the driveway, as she does every Saturday.

At the grocery store she helps me navigate the sea of choices by reading nutrition labels, weights, sizes, flavors, and prices, among other things. At the craft store, she reads the fiber content, yardage, color, weight, and price of the various yarns, making sure that I get sufficient yarn from the same dye lot. Selecting the correct size and length for knitting needles would be impossible without her help.

This weekly shopping routine allows us to get together, have some lunch, enjoy each other's company, and maintain a friendship with roots in a previous generation.

WALLY HINZ

Back in the Swing of Things

When I came back to Vision Loss Resources in 1996, one of my instructors said to me, "Did you ever play golf when you could see? I have some information on golf for people with disabilities at Braemar golf course out in Edina. Would you be interested?"

I filled out the paperwork but then I had to find someone who would be willing to work with me. I called my old friend Terry and asked him, "Would you be willing to help me?" "Sure," he said. A month later the phone rang and he asked, "You got your clubs close by? Your shoes? I'm gonna be there in twenty minutes to pick you up. We're gonna find out what kind of a (bleep-bleep) athlete you really are."

Twenty minutes later, we headed for Somerset Country Club in St. Paul where Terry was a member, picked up a great big bucket of practice balls, and headed for the practice range. He and I had never played golf together when I could see, so he had no idea what kind of swing I had. We also had to figure out how a sighted instructor works with a blind student.

I got into my stance and took a swing, and he critiqued my swing.

We started hitting 8 irons, and after each swing he'd tell me where the ball went and how far. After a dozen or so, we switched to a 5 iron. After the tenth swing, I heard only dead silence. No critique—nothing. What happened?

"Wally, the head of your 5 iron is about twenty yards out in front of us. You just broke your 5 iron."

I started to laugh. They weren't expensive clubs.

We switched to the 4 wood. I had mud and grass on the sole of my left shoe. When I reached down to clean off the shoe, the sole came off in my hand. We both laughed.

I had broken an iron and destroyed my shoes. I said to him, "I think it might be time to hang it up."

As we put the clubs back, my buddy asked, "Did you have that slice when you could see?"

"Yeah, why?"

"Hinz, the blindness is not your problem. You're a lousy golfer."

That was the beginning of our playing golf together, and we then went on to play for about fourteen years at the regulation course at Braemar in Edina with a regular foursome. The other disabled person in the foursome, Jim Dodge, was paralyzed from the waist down. He played off of a special cart. The guy had a great game. One day we played eighteen holes and my paralyzed buddy shot a 99. I shot a 102 that day, so I had to buy dinner for Jim because he won. We played together up until Jim died. The rest of us still play together and rotate courses in the Twin Cities and up in Moose Lake, where Jim was from.

Every year I play in my high school alumni tournament. It's the shotgun start, scramble format. A few years ago, I was playing in a foursome with Tony Pazik, Tom Kozlak, and the coach Bill Horning. We teed off on hole 14, so we finished up on 13, where one of the golf pros was. It's a par 3, 185 yards, and you pay $5 if you want to try to beat the pro off the tee.

Tom Kozlak challenged the pro: "I got five bucks that says you can't beat Wally off the tee."

The pro didn't respond.

Then Tom said, "I've got ten bucks that says you can't beat Wally."

The pro said, "OK, you're on."

I hit my shot to the edge of the green.

The pro started to walk up to the tee, and Tom said, "I don't think you understand what I said. If you're gonna beat Wally off the tee, you have to play golf the same way he does."

They wrapped a towel around his head. The pro duffed two or three shots. Horning was howling with laughter.

Afterward, at dinner, they made the announcement: "Wally beat the pro off the tee."

A year later, I was playing in the same tournament. We teed off on 14, so the last hole was again on 13.

As I walked toward the tee, I encountered the same pro. He sauntered over to me and said, "I've been waiting a year for you, buddy."

Golf has been a lot of fun for me. Frankly, I'm playing better golf since I lost my sight than I did when I could see.

HELEN BARTLETT

In Lieu of Crosswords

Fading vision
Made the decision
Since I can no longer view
The puzzles that I do
Words playing in my head
Write poetry instead

SUE OLSON

Storytime

In 2004, I was enrolled in a program that I'll call "blindschool." The teachers taught braille, computer, keyboarding, and home economics. They also taught travel and mobility—how to get around town and take city buses.

I stopped by the store to pick up some groceries, because a winter storm was coming and I wanted to stock up on food and necessities in case I couldn't get out for a few days.

As day became evening, I still had a thirty- to forty-minute commute home. The wind was swirling snow around and the cold stung my cheeks. I boarded my bus safely and was about halfway home when suddenly a strong smell of smoke filled the bus. We stopped quickly on the side of the highway. The bus driver told us to evacuate the bus and wait on the shoulder. It was very cold and windy with minus-forty windchill. Some places the snow was knee-high.

After a few minutes that seemed much longer, the driver said it was safe to get back on the bus. Within minutes the emergency lights went out and we were in total darkness with no heat. The bus driver explained that it could be several hours before a backup bus would arrive. As time passed, people were feeling cold, hungry, and restless. Little kids were crying. I, too, longed for my warm bed, hot cocoa, and a hot shower. Then it hit me. I had an idea.

"Let's have a party," I suggested. "I have some snacks that I'll share with you. I have some bottled water, trail mix, chips, and Oreos. If everybody shares, we'll have enough. I can even entertain you by reading."

A guy stood up and complained, "Duh, no lights."

I replied, "I don't need any. I'm blind and can read braille."

I started reading from the book I had with me, *Little House on the Prairie*. Nobody complained when I goofed up a word or two. I explained that I was just learning.

I was on my sixth page when our rescue bus showed up. Cheers and yeahs abounded. Some people gave me money. A lot of people shook my hand and said, "Thanks!" It felt good to make a winter evening a little less cold. I sure was happy when I walked through my front door, even when my daughter complained that I forgot the Oreos.

DENA WAINWRIGHT

Memories of Rae

When I was nineteen years old, I decided it was time to get my first guide dog. A few months earlier, my best friend, Kathryn, had been paired with a beautiful, black and red German shepherd, and she now seemed so much more independent and confident. My parents, not wanting to admit that their first-born child was growing up, were less than enthusiastic about the idea of me flying across the continent to attend the four-week training program. They were probably also nervous about the idea that a short, furry creature would be responsible for my safety. Nevertheless, after filling out the application forms, completing the in-home visits, and asking myself if I was really ready to care for another living thing, I received word that I had been accepted to a guide dog school in California. My training was to begin on March 28, 1993.

When I got off the plane in San Francisco, I was greeted by one of my guide dog instructors, who packed me and my luggage into a bus full of other students for the thirty-minute ride to the school's San Rafael campus. The campus was beautiful: manicured lawns, walking paths, and tall trees surrounding a student dormitory, administration building, and huge dog kennel.

As I looked around my room, the impending arrival of my new dog became very real. A tiled area below my bathroom sink contained a faucet and an empty water dish. A fleece mat rested on the floor beside my bed and a brand-new leather leash waited on my desk. I didn't know how I was going to contain my excitement until my meeting with my mystery companion.

Three days of pre-dog preparation taught us how to issue commands to invisible animals, dole out praise, administer fair punishments, and work with leather dog harnesses. Finally the magical day arrived. I sat in the lecture room with my classmates and waited to hear the name, breed, and gender of my new partner. When my turn came, I was told that I would be receiving a female German shepherd named Rae. After we had learned the basics about our new dogs, we were sent back to our rooms to wait.

I watched anxiously as my fellow students walked down the long, tiled hall, disappearing into the instructors' office and emerging minutes later with their new dogs at their sides. After what seemed like hours, my turn finally came. I was led into the same office and settled into an oversized armchair.

"Are you ready to meet Rae?" my instructor asked.

I nodded, as the door to the outside run was opened and sixty-five pounds of fur with pointy ears flew across the room and landed at my feet.

My hands moved over her slim, athletic body—her sculpted face, her bushy tail, and her enormous ears. As I did this, my instructor described Rae's elaborate markings to me.

I left in a haze of joy, Rae plodding expectantly beside me. Like all first-time dog handlers, I was thinking that my dog was the most perfect dog ever and that we would be the best of friends from this moment on. To my dismay, it didn't happen quite so easily.

When we returned to my room, I sat down on the floor with Rae, thinking we could get in some cuddle time before I had to feed her and take her out to relieve herself. Rae, however, only had eyes for her trainer. When he would walk by my open door, she would wail and strain at her leash in an attempt to reach him. I quickly revised my "best of friends" scenario and decided I'd be happy with her liking me even just a little.

When it came time to feed her, she wouldn't eat. When I took her outside, she just looked at me, flattened her ears, and sat unmoving at my feet.

Again, like all first-time dog handlers whose dogs don't perform according to their expectations, I became convinced that my dog hated me. I said as much to my instructor, who reassured me and told me to "give it time."

The next morning, after a night plagued with self-doubts and little sleep, Rae and I took our first walk together. I will never forget that walk. Until then, I had no idea that it was possible to move that quickly or gracefully through space. We virtually flew two blocks, before Rae even looked up at me.

My instructor laughed at the expression of surprise that came over Rae's intelligent, little face when she finally noticed that I was the one who was holding onto the harness. It was like she was thinking, "Oh, I didn't realize you were attached to me. Where's the person I usually walk with?"

It has been more than twenty years since that California spring day. I have had the privilege of working with several other dogs since then, and though each has touched my heart, none will ever replace Rae. During my time with Rae, I changed from a girl to a woman. With Rae, I got my bachelor of arts degree and became a dotcomer. With Rae, I rode in a stretch limousine through Manhattan and in a canoe over a set of white water rapids in northern Canada. With Rae, I fell in love, fell out of it, and fell in love again.

The relationship that a person has with their guide is so difficult to explain. It's a combination of parent/child, partner, and friend. Rae gave me immeasurable gifts. She taught me about unconditional love and what it feels like to literally owe your life to another living soul. She licked my tears away when I cried and stood regally beside me when I was successful. She was my light, my heart, my wings, and the key to my independence.

With my boundless gratitude, this story is for her.

ROBERT ANDERSON

Turnabout

The Minnesota Twins had just won the 1987 World Series, and crowds were beginning to mass along the motorcade route near the State Capitol. Tens of thousands of jubilant fans were expected on this bright, crisp October afternoon. Not even a fair-weather baseball fan, I left work early to avoid the crush, but the sidewalks were already jammed, and I soon found myself tapping my white stick through a dense thicket of humanity.

"This is no place for a blind man," I thought, zigzagging and excusing my way through the crowd until I stalled, boxed in, my cane crushed against my chest.

"Can I help?" A hand touched my arm.

"Yeah, I'm stuck."

The stranger, a raspy whisper on my right, began to steer me by the elbow, gently at first, then more firmly, directing me toward thin spots in the crowd.

"Make way for the blind man, make way for the blind man!" he shouted as he propelled me through the almost impenetrable mass. When even he got stuck, he squeezed behind me and began shoving hard with both hands against the small of my back, forcing my hips forward, pivoting them left and right with his fingertips, thrusting my trunk forward and driving it like a wedge through the mob. Helpless on my own, I surrendered.

"Make way for the blind man, make way for the blind man!" we both yelled as I raised my cane high and waved it aloft like a pennant. With each advance, the crowd congealed around us, but my friend drove all the harder, twisting my body to test resistance and jamming it into every fissure and fault line he could find.

We made a curious conga line that clear October afternoon as we snaked our way up the long avenue toward the Capitol. Near the crest of the hill, the crowd began to thin and our momentum accelerated until, suddenly, with one final shove, we popped through to the other side, free at last, as cleanly expressed as a squeezed carbuncle.

"Thank you, thank you!" I gushed. "I could never have done it without you."

"No, no, thank *you*!" He extended his hand. "I've got a dentist's appointment in twenty minutes, and if I hurry, I can just make it."

JOHN PRIESTLEY

Bus Ride

This is a true story of something that happened on a Minneapolis bus.

My name is John Priestley, and my guide dog was Kylo, a 103-pound yellow Lab. One afternoon we were taking the bus home to Plymouth. We boarded the bus and sat across from the driver. The same people were on the bus as every day, and we greeted them as we got on. But on this day a woman who was new to the bus was on and I greeted her. She didn't know I have vision loss.

She asked what kind of guide dog I had. I thought a minute and responded that it was a black Lab! She looked down at my yellow Lab and was stunned! She looked at me, then back to my yellow Lab and looked at me again and just then the people on the bus started laughing!

I told her if you don't have a sense of humor, then you might as well pack it in!

DIANE O'SHAUGHNESSY

Who Was That Girl?

C onsider this story as a silly but true situation comedy about my friend Colleen and me, Diane, out to lunch (for sure) one afternoon in a dark restaurant. I have night blindness, which Colleen thinks is just a hoot. Let's face it; sometimes it can be very funny.

Colleen O'Hara is my bright-eyed Irish friend who is so much fun to be with—SOMETIMES. The only problem is that she thinks EVERYTHING is funny, no matter what it is! There is also a young businessman who enters into the situation. Let's call him "the guy who tried to help."

You know how they say, "You just had to be there"? Well, in this case, you had to have been there. So, I will place you there. Imagine that you are the onlooker, the young businessman. You play a vital role in this comedy of errors. You are a star!

It's a bright, sunny day. Your morning business went well and you are feeling good. You decide to take your favorite, pretty secretary out to lunch at a popular local restaurant, and you are looking for a corner table in the back, where it will be quiet so you can have a relaxing, romantic, strictly no-business lunch. But this is not going to happen today. The hostess sits the two of you down right in the middle by the main aisle, next to a couple of giggling middle-aged gals. (That would be Colleen, the brunette, and me, the blonde.)

So, you hear the blonde ask the brunette where the ladies' room is, and the brunette says, "Right straight back there, down the aisle." Next, you see the blonde weave her way down the aisle and, of course, you think she had one too many, but you don't know that she can't see well, because she is not carrying a blind cane. (Why would she do that anyway? She doesn't need one yet; and, if she were to use one, well, then people might think she can't see, and that would be so embarrassing.)

You are incredulous as you watch this girl walk straight into the men's room, and at the same time you spot the brunette quietly snickering at her table. But you haven't noticed your favorite secretary seething as she is wondering why you are ogling the brunette and the blonde.

Now you decide that you *must* let that girl know that she has wandered into no-woman's land. You excuse yourself and walk into the men's room, and all you see is a small pair of high heels in a men's stall.

You clear your throat and mumble, "Hmmm . . . I must be in the wrong men's room."

With horror, she hears your voice and spots your large men's shoes standing there, right there, in *her* bathroom. Then she, in her snobbiest voice says, "Well, I *guess* you are!"

So you say, "Oops, I'm sorry. I'll look for the other men's room," and you leave, hoping that she got the hint.

She, however, is still not the least bit aware that *she* was in the wrong place. She comes out of the stall, spins around the corner to find a sink, and wonders why the sinks are so low.

"*Oh no!*" is all she can say. She has to get out of there. But how? How can she sneak out of there and fly into the ladies' room without all those people in the restaurant seeing her?

You are back at your table now waiting for the inevitable to happen. The next thing you see is the men's door opening just a crack. You see this little nose peeking out ever so sneakily.

She must have stayed like that for three minutes, trying to make sure the hallway was empty and trying to read which door actually says "Women." She couldn't read it, as, of course, she doesn't have her glasses on. They are homely and Coke-bottle thick, and if she wore them out to lunch, she would look silly, and that would also be embarrassing. She thinks, "Where is Colleen? Doesn't she know that after all this time, I am in some kind of trouble? She *must* be in the ladies' room waiting for me. She knows that I will *not* be re-entering this restaurant, knowing that these people most likely saw what I did. How can I escape from here without anyone seeing me? And where the heck is the ladies' room?" Upon peeking out once again, she sees a door straight across the hall. That's got to be it.

You are really curious now and can't wait until the blonde comes back to the table so you can give her a "Ha Ha" wink, as in "I don't know who you are, but I saw what you did."

Just as your favorite secretary, your romantic lunch date, is becoming increasingly stressed at your apparent dismissal of her, you dismiss her yet again as your jaw drops at the sight of the blonde launching herself out of the men's room and across the hallway, directly into the kitchen. You notice that her friend is watching also, with more than just a snicker this time. You wonder just *when* this "friend" is going to go and rescue her pal.

It's me, again, Diane. I'm in the kitchen. I'm in the gol-danged kitchen! A very short, but assertive, little man looks at me like I have antennae sticking out of my head.

Then, having a second thought, I guess he says in his best broken English, "Vas your foot not goot?"

"What?" I say. "No. No. I don't know. I haven't had a chance to eat yet. Sorry. I'm sorry. I'm in the wrong room again."

"What chu lookin' for?" he says.

"The ladies' room. Please! Where is the ladies' room?"

"Over der, across da hall," he replies.

"Oh no, it's not; trust me. I have already been there."
Now I'm getting really flustered.

Then he points at another exit door from the kitchen. "Out der. Over der."

"Thank God," I moan. So I find the door and proceed to push it open, although it actually was aligned to pull open with a large metal handle. That hurt.

OK. Now you are baffled that you have not yet seen the blonde exit the room that you know is the kitchen. You are speculating, "What the heck? Did she find lunch in there?"

You finally decide to eat your lunch and stop worrying about the dingbat in the kitchen. Your favorite, pretty secretary is ecstatic. Now, back to the business of flirting with her. All is going well, when, out of the corner of your eye, you see the blonde charge out of the kitchen and run across to yet another room. You choke on your sip of wine and it comes out your nose as you break out in laughter. You share your laughter with the brunette prankster at the other table, but not with your clueless secretary, who thinks that you and the brunette are having way too much fun. The bemused secretary stands up, wipes herself off, casually places her cloth napkin over your head and walks out. This day is just not working out as planned.

Well, here I am, finally in the ladies' room. I am not leaving this room until Colleen comes to get me. Another five minutes go by. No Colleen. I know what happened. She probably saw some of my shenani-gans and is embarrassed to be seen with me. That's a fine how-do-you-do. OK. I'm leaving. I think the glass doors are right around the corner . . . I hope. I open the door and run around the corner, out the glass doors. To my utter amazement, there sits Colleen, curled up in the corner on the floor, holding her stomach and laughing hysterically. Why am I surprised? This is my wild Irish friend whom I know and love in spite of herself.

After a minute or so, she finally blurts out, "It's OK, I paid the bill."

"That's just dandy" I say, "being as you actually got to eat lunch."

You are frantic. You can't find your waitress, and you need to pay up and get out. You have to chase down your secretary and apologize. You are just about ready to dash when the waitress finally shows up with your bill. Soon you run down the hallway and blast through the glass doors. Now you are speechless, as you see those two twits . . . the ones who ruined your day . . . the blonde and the brunette, sitting in the corner, on the floor together, belly laughing. All you can think is, "Have I just been punk'd by the Girls Behaving Badly team?"

"Women!" is the only thing you mutter as you begin running again.

BEV HAALAND-SAVAGE

Talent

Kerri is a volunteer reader assigned to me by Vision Loss Resources. She arrives at my house every other Saturday to process all of the bills, bank statements, notes I've received, notes I need to write, and so on. After we do those, we get to the important stuff. You know, shopping online. Yup, shopping online. You see, I have a talking computer. It is an ordinary computer equipped with a speaking screen reader called JAWS. This program reads what is on the screen with great accuracy and detail.

On a recent Saturday I had found a delightful item of interest I thought I might like to order—"touch of lace tee shirt"—but I wanted Kerri's opinion and some additional information about it. I turned the screen toward her and asked her to take a look at the shirt.

"Beverly, your screen is upside down. *How did you do that?*" she exclaimed.

"Talent, Kerri, talent. You have no idea the computer talent I possess," I replied.

"Well," she said, "it's making me dizzy." Then she added, "Wait a minute, what if I turn the mouse upside down? Bingo!" she cried.

Well, I got my "touch of lace tee shirt," and so it was

another very good day. I have no idea how I turned the screen upside down and I have no idea how to get it back right side up.

I love my computer. Wait, how do I erase this? What I mean is I have found a lot to like about being dragged kicking and screaming into the twenty-first century.

ERIN E. C. SALINAS

Living with Vision Loss North and South of the Border

When I was working at a community-based re-habilitation center in a rural Mexican town seven years ago, I met a young man I'll call Emilio. He had been blind since infancy and came from a well-to-do family in a neighboring town. Unlike most persons with disabilities we served, he had been fortunate enough to obtain an education. His family chose to hire private tutors, as the public special education system left much to be desired. He had soaked up his education, supplementing it by listening to the radio avidly. He often asked me questions about English, having picked up a few phrases from the radio.

While his family had done their best, they had created a bubble for him without realizing it. He had no activities of his own, only going out with family. He had no plans for employment, and needless to say, no social life of his own, despite being an adolescent. Family members always led him around, linking their arms with his. As limiting as this may sound, people considered him very fortunate—at least his family allowed him to come out of the house and let him obtain an education. Many parents with disabled children kept them indoors most of their lives because they felt ashamed; society viewed the children's disability as proof that the parents had caused it by committing a horrible sin.

When Emilio arrived at the rehab center where I worked, the staff gave him a bamboo pole to use as a cane, as there were no white canes. They introduced him to the two other blind teenagers, and he started to learn to use the cane. A few weeks later, knowing that I was going to visit my family in Minnesota, a friend suggested that I contact Vision Loss Resources to ask them to donate some equipment. I don't recall the name of the person who gave me several canes and Spanish-speaking devices, but I remember that her generosity impressed me. Emilio and the other clients were thrilled with their new canes.

As an occupational therapist at the rehab center, I sought employment opportunities for our clients, but I had limited success with placement. While we would start to make progress on their skill development, for some reason we would come to a standstill. But Emilio was an exception. We began working on bread making and he showed great enthusiasm for it, churning out muffins and whole-wheat loaves. He even asked me to help him look up new recipes. After I left the center, my friends, who had stayed behind, reported that Emilio continued to make bread on his own and with other clients. Finally, I had been able to teach at least one person a skill, and he was able to continue without me. Still, I wasn't too optimistic about his future employment prospects because when we had gone out to promote our bread to local businesses for wholesale purchases, most said that they would be interested in buying only during the high season. Unfortunately, the high season only lasted a few weeks out of the year. Although Emilio had learned a trade, he had no support in living an independent life outside the center. Usually, he and other disabled clients had to resort to singing on public buses in nearby Oaxaca City, a step up from placing their caps on the sidewalks to beg for money.

Years later, while planning to move back to Minnesota, I came across an employment ad for a community services specialist at Vision Loss Resources. The ad mentioned connecting clients to community resources and working with a diverse clientele. At my interview, the person asked if I would like to work with Latino clients, since I speak Spanish. "Wonderful," I thought. "I can finally help this population in a place where the community will support them more—Minnesota, land of unbridled volunteerism and 10,000 nonprofits," or so it seemed to me coming back from Mexico.

I thoroughly enjoy my work as a community services specialist. I love the look of joy on my clients' faces when I tell them about programs or resources to help them. They say, "You mean I can still . . . ?" Most of them are from economically challenged areas of Mexico, and I can imagine their ideas about what it means to have vision loss. They probably recall the blind persons they have seen singing on buses or placing their caps on the sidewalk. My clients with vision loss often tell me they can't do much of anything anymore, but at least they can rely on their families to help them. When I ask them whether they're interested in relearning skills to become independent, they often shrug because they are unfamiliar with the concept. Once they experience a few of our tricks with adaptive techniques or adaptive equipment, they are amazed and thrilled at the possibilities.

Yet, even if they understand that it's possible to relearn skills despite their vision loss, they encounter other barriers. For instance, some don't speak English, some lack an understanding of American systems, and some are poor. On the bright side, however, they usually have a lot of family support, which tends to be more highly valued in Latino culture than it is in mainstream American culture. Those without family resources truly rely on our services. An example is one of my clients, who is nearly blind due to diabetic retinopathy and is on dialysis three times a week. He was thrilled when I taught him how to walk with a long white cane, and when I set him up with Metro Mobility, the TED phone program, and a volunteer reader.

I maintain that there are great things about both

Mexican and American cultures, but I am happy to be able to introduce some clients to one of the things I appreciate about American culture: having a disability doesn't necessarily mean giving up one's independence. Whatever level of independent living they choose, at least they will have more options in the United States than they will have many other places. My daydreams involve the whole world having access to an organization like Vision Loss Resources when they are affected by disabilities. But, for now, I'll just keep reaching out to one client at a time.

LINDA LEANGER

Hearing Voices

We have many voices in our home—all competing for attention. We have talking watches, talking clocks, a talking computer, talking recorders, a talking caller ID, a talking thermostat, and oh yes, a talking alarm clock named Moshi. We are convinced that when we leave the house, all of these talking devices hold meetings, plotting against us on how they can confound us.

Our thermostat will often ignore us, but it will answer Charlie (our cocker spaniel) when he barks, announcing to him the time and temperature—as if he cares.

Once I had a talking watch that had a crowing rooster as an alarm. Sometimes the alarm would get set inadvertently. So, in my nightmarish imagination, one day I would be sitting in church on a Sunday morning, and the alarm would be set at 12:00. Just at the time the pastor would be winding up his message, the alarm would go off, with twelve repetitions of a rooster crowing. I would try to bury the watch under layers of sweaters, a coat, a purse, books, and so on. Meanwhile I would gaze ahead with rapt attention, oblivious to any commotion going on around me. But alas! My red face would give me away.

As if my talking watch is not bad enough, Moshi, my talking alarm clock, is a real pest. When we say, "Hello, Moshi," she answers: "Welcome. Command, please." (My husband suggests I address him in a similar manner. She gives him ideas like that!) If we answer the phone in the same room as Moshi, she often butts in on our conversation with "Welcome. Command, please." As if she knows what we are talking about. If we ignore her, she will say, "Sorry, I did not recognize your command." She always interrupts when I am listening to a book on my recorder— trying to get attention. If I ignore her, she selects her own prompt, such as choosing a "sleep sound" so I have to listen to my book with birds chirping in the background. Then, when we want her to speak, she often gives us the silent treatment. She must be "put out" about something.

The other day my husband was trying to adjust the time with Moshi, and I heard him muttering, "She just doesn't get it." I talked a friend into getting Moshi, and now Moshi is driving her crazy, too. Why should my friend live in peace and quiet?

After all of Moshi's interruptions, I decided to try working with a male voice for JAWS, my screen reader. But he has proved to be a real jerk. Why should I trust him? He lies a lot. He likes to stick his nose in my life. When spell-checking text that includes my last name, Leanger, he suggests I be "leaner." I suggest he mind his own business. Often, when I'm on the phone,

JAWS starts interrupting, so I have to explain to the caller why they are hearing another voice speaking. He really annoys me by fixating on some part of the screen that I am not interested in, repeating it over and over. Finally, I have to silence him by pressing the control key, or I must move him to the part of the screen I want him to read; this is done by key commands.

He really enjoys setting me up for embarrassing experiences—like when our pastor stopped in for a visit. At an opportune moment, JAWS started chattering behind closed doors. I felt it necessary to introduce our pastor to JAWS, lest he suspect I was attempting to conceal another man in the house.

And then there are screen savers. Once I had a jungle theme. I had just picked up the phone when the screen saver started playing the sound of a trumpeting elephant. I had to convince the caller that I really did not have an elephant in my office. Thank God it wasn't playing the Tarzan yell; imagine trying to explain that one.

If, when you see me, my sanity comes into question, please realize I have been hearing a lot of voices.

LINDA WALTZ

Apostle Island Sea Cave Adventure

In late August of 2012, we were all hunkered down in our sleeping bags for the first night of our Apostle Island sea kayak trip with Wilderness Inquiry on Lake Superior. I felt safe tucked in my tent between Kate, the fearless leader of Vision Loss Resources, and Barry, her partner, in their tent on one side, and Clancy, our fearless leader of Wilderness Inquiry (WI), in his hammock between two trees on the other. The guide rope along the hike to the privy was the last puzzle piece for independence and dignity. Connecting my cane tip to the overhead guide rope produced a fun trolley experience. I could walk along it as fast as I travel with my dog guide, and that made me very happy. Everything seemed perfect as I lay restfully wide awake.

Two people per four-person tent was blissful. My tent mate, Nancy, was dead to the world in three minutes flat, and that made everything groovy. I sighed appreciatively as I snuggled deeper into the soft fleece liner within my sleeping bag on top of the heavy extra sleeping bag I brought to put over the WI-issued sleep mat. Being familiar with the skimpiness of the

WI mat, I brought extra cushion to appease my inner princess, since we were base camping.

As I soaked in the stillness and amazing quiet, I pondered how God had answered my heart's desire for this experience. My first challenge was leaving my dog guide behind. He was left in good hands, as were the cats and my home. My second challenge was met after I had received permission from WI to bring my own cooler stocked with foods suitable for my food allergies and sensitivities. All the pieces had fallen very nicely into place, and all was well with my inner princess.

My peaceful thoughts were interrupted by the rainstorm. There was no wind, and the storm was significant without being torrential. The occasional gentle rumble of thunder lulled me.

Very early that Thursday morning, nine clients of Vision Loss Resources' community center had loaded our gear into a trailer and ourselves into the Wilderness Inquiry van. We ranged in varying degrees of vision loss, kayak experience, and familiarity with our team members. I, along with two others, was without eyesight or kayak experience. The van was piloted by Clancy and Hannah, two WI staff. Three Vision Loss Resources volunteers drove separately, allowing for as many clients as possible to make the long trip comfortably in the van to Little Sand Bay Base Camp on the Bayfield Peninsula of Wisconsin.

After our arrival, we had gathered in a circle to introduce ourselves with our wishes for the trip. Then we had toured the warehouse and had been issued our wet suits, life jackets, and sleep mats. We loaded our gear in a cart and hiked into camp, which seemed to be a small natural clearing in the midst of a vast wilderness. I liked that the tents were set up on knee-high platforms. While we entered and set up camp with little direction, we all seemed to fold together naturally into a cohesive and cooperative community. Even though I disliked the tip test we did after setting up camp, I knew that if, God forbid, my kayak tipped, I would easily bob to the surface like a cork. "Let it rain all it wants tonight," I sighed contentedly. "There will be blue skies smiling at me in the morning." Eventually I drifted off.

I was awakened by the chatter of early morning birds. It is a slow and arduous process for me to awake to full consciousness and friendly interaction in the morning. "Well," I mumbled as I drew deep inside my sleeping bag. "There seems to be a definite disadvantage to being in one of the two tents with the food station and tables in front of them." I surrendered and moved slowly, preparing to greet the morning and my team members as I considered my greatest challenge of the trip. I am an introvert. I am easily overwhelmed in large groups and multiple conversations in said groups, especially early in the morning. I was pleased to find that even this greatest challenge was manageable in this small community as we grew in appreciation and support of one another.

We spent Friday morning paddling around in a quiet bay off of Lake Superior. My preference was to have my kayak experience free of the ankle-to-shoulder wet suit and the kayak skirt. We only needed the life jacket in this quiet bay. The water was as still as glass in this bay and so much warmer than Lake Superior itself. At one point we could hear the roar of the waves of Lake Superior in the distance. It sounded like the ocean. I absorbed the beauty and blissful stillness surrounding me. I considered the wonders of what God had wrought in this space undefiled by industry and technology as I trailed my hand in the water to feel the large lily pads.

After our time on the water, we made our way to a beachside park for lunch. It was there I fulfilled my wish to swim in Lake Superior unencumbered by the dreaded wet suit or shoes. The bay of this beach park was shallow, with the depth increasing ever so gradually. It took a long walk to get deep enough to dive under safely. It was so warm. It was glorious.

From there we made our way into Bayfield, a very quaint and quiet town, where some of us shopped and some of us sat in a rooftop lounge overlooking the lake. Then it was back to camp for supper, campfire conversation, and early bedtime. Once again I was lulled to sleep by the rain, feeling deeply grateful and appreciative of the gift of another day safe and secure in the wilderness.

We hung out at camp the next morning, hoping for the winds to die down. After lunch in a park at the top of the bluff above Meyers Beach, it was time to squeeze ourselves into those dreaded wet suits and bulky life jackets.

Barry was the bowman in the front of the voyager canoe, the one who sets the rowing pace to keep everyone in sync. Nancy and I shared the seat behind him. Behind us, three of our team members balanced us. Captain Clancy steered from the rear. We pushed off shore for the experience of a lifetime. Barry kept us in stitches with his calls, as we all seemed to bore quickly of, "Stroke, stroke, stroke, and stroke." Soon it became different foods and beverages, from category to category.

All at once I heard Clancy say, "Okay, stop paddling," and we made a sharp right turn into a sea cave. We passed through a veil into a wonder of ancient magic and mystery. We all heeded Clancy's directions on cue throughout our magical mystery tour in the caves. "Oars in. Oars out. Oars in. Paddle forward. Paddle back. Duck." He maneuvered that enormous canoe like a sports car. He directed it in such a way that at times we created a crashing wave, using the sound to measure the size of each cave. Each gasp of amazement sounded out more fully the shape and size of the caves. He brought the canoe right next to cave walls so we could touch them, and in places we could touch the roof of the cave. It was the most amazing experience to feel those cave walls and realize they had been carved by the same water we floated in. Albert Einstein said that everything is energy. I am highly sensitive to the vibration and frequency of that energy. I felt the life force of God vibrating through those cave walls, which seemed to hold some hidden and silent life wisdom I wanted to absorb.

We then came to a tunnel leading out of the caves that I still cannot believe our captain piloted that large boat through. "Okay," he directed us. "Oars in and duck down as low as you can go." We folded ourselves in half. We could reach up and touch the roof and the walls at the same time as we inched through the very long tunnel. The energy of our amazement and excitement synergistically filled the tunnel and illuminated it. When we finally emerged into the warm sunlight, I raised my arms in the air and squealed and hooted my excitement. It was absolutely exhilarating. "Do you want to do it again?" he asked when I paused to catch my breath. "Yes! Yes! Yes!" I screamed. "Let's do it again." It was even more thrilling the second time. Even now, writing this a year later, I once again am filled from head to toe with excitement.

Too soon for me it was time to head back to Meyers Beach. We hailed our captain Clancy, shouting his praises for the thrill of the sea caves adventure almost all the way back to the dock. His name became our stroking call for rhythm. I can still hear the laughter and feel the joy.

Around the campfire that night, we shared the greatest highlight of our trip. Mine was definitely the experience in the sea caves. My greatest wish for the trip had been fulfilled. Clancy brought a WI staff member to serenade us with his banjo. We clapped and stomped our feet to the music and hooted our appreciation. It was the perfect closing for a perfectly amazing trip. It was so much fun!

In my sleeping nest that night I was overflowing with gratitude and appreciation. I drifted off quickly and easily, marveling at how free I felt, safe in the heart of God. I surely didn't want to leave. Every single memory is a glistening treasure as it passes through like water glancing off a paddle wheel. Each droplet of experience still sparkles like a facet of a diamond. I feel richly blessed beyond measure for my wilderness experience. My heart and soul expand as I cherish each and every moment. As I have unpacked and reflected on this amazing journey of self-discovery amidst natural wonder, I hear the words of the song "The Time of My Life" from the movie *Dirty Dancing*. I would compare the thrill of being led on a wilderness experience by Clancy Ray of Wilderness Inquiry to dancing with Patrick Swayze.

I surely did have the time of my life on my Apostle Island Sea Cave adventure.

DIANE O'SHAUGHNESSY

Taking a Chance on Dance

Dancing is beauty and grace, and excitement. It lifts the spirit and lightens the heart. I think my passion for dance is in the genes, because my mother (bless her soul), as a young lady, was a dancer. She used to dance and sing, performing at some local public venues in the St. Paul area, and so she made sure I got the tap and ballet lessons as a young girl.

I took a jazz class when I was in my twenties, and I always wanted to take ballroom dancing lessons, but as life goes, I somehow managed to be in relationships with men who thought dancing was for sissies. So, I didn't get involved in ballroom dancing until I was fifty-eight years old. Then, I was a single lady and heard about a new place in Woodbury called the Tropical Ballroom. Luckily, I had a neighbor and friend who wanted to try it too, so we went there. Actually, we were two of their first students. My vision was pretty bad by then, but I just had to try.

I really had no idea how much fun it would be. My instructor, James Wood, was a fabulous dancer. He was hilariously funny and an excellent teacher. I warned him that I had very little peripheral vision and that his dealing with me could become somewhat tedious, but he said, "Don't worry, you will dance just fine with me." He proved what a warm heart and a little patience could do for a person with a handicap. We did very well together.

Occasionally, when he would swing me out, I would just keep on going. One time, as I swung back to him, the first two fingers on my swinging left hand landed directly in his mouth. Another time, he got a judo chop right across the neck. His reaction? He always laughed and joked about it.

Some of the other guys in the group didn't really want to dance with me, as there were other girls they felt safer with (go figure). But when James saw me standing alone, sometimes he would come over and be my partner.

I experienced the shock of my life on the day he asked me to be his partner in a Viennese waltz dance showcase at the ballroom. This is one of the most beautiful dances I've ever seen and, by far, my favorite. I couldn't believe he was asking me, and I replied, "James, I could never do that." He replied, "Oh yes you can, if you do it with me. Just dance like nobody's watching." And so we choreographed the dance, practiced for a few weeks, and voilà! Suddenly, there we were. He wore a phantom-type black outfit, with a sleek black eye mask, and I wore a gorgeous, long blue gown, swaying and whirling around the ballroom floor to the lovely rhythm of a Viennese waltz. We ended the dance with a curtsy and a bow, and the audience clapped and cameras flashed. It was surreal to me . . . like a dream come true. Mom, are you watching?

Today, my dancing is limited, as my vision has deteriorated substantially, and my inability to see in the dark has pretty much turned group lessons into a circus, with me as the clown. However, where there's a will, there's a way. I found a dance studio in Minneapolis called the Social Dance Studio, where they offer five-dollar, one-hour dance lessons to seniors every morning of the week. I love the waltz and the tango, so I go there once or twice a week. The windows in the ballroom make it just bright enough for me to navigate without destroying something. That large pillar in the center of the room has now become my adversary.

The owners are zany and fun, all the instructors are great, and the senior dancers are kind and accepting of my occasional mishaps. I am forever grateful for these dance experiences and to those who helped me along the way. Here's hoping that I can continue on just a little bit longer.

JEAN CHRISTY

Crossroads: One-Hundredth Anniversary Thoughts

I have worked at Vision Loss Resources for about thirty years in three different positions, but they have all been in the direct services section of the agency. I still enjoy my work due to the remarkable people I have had the chance to know throughout the years.

I have worked with people from eighteen different countries.

I have worked with a person who grew up in rural Mississippi in the '60s and did not remember ever going to school, and I have worked with 3M scientists who were using low-vision devices to read twenty-five-letter words I had never heard before.

I have worked with people who were priests, nuns, and other clergy. And I have worked with people who were former felons from both property and violent crimes.

I have worked with people who were homeless while attending the program and people who had more money than they could spend in a lifetime.

I have worked with brand-new immigrants who did

not speak English and people who were new to "the Cities" because they had never been out of their rural Minnesota communities.

I have worked with people who identify as straight and people who identify as gay and one male who dressed as a female while waiting for a sex-change operation.

I have worked with people who were atheists and people who had strict religious beliefs that dictated fully covered dress and requests for same-sex instructors. I have worked with people who were born blind and clients who lost all of their vision instantaneously later in life. I have worked with people who became blind from genetic diseases, tragic accidents, and gunshots, whether accidental or purposeful or self-inflicted. I have worked with people who were blinded as a result of torture and one person who gouged out his own eyes while in prison.

The commonality throughout the numerous clients' histories is vision loss. Vision Loss Resources is neither the beginning of the road nor the end of the road, but a rejuvenating crossroads for clients along the way. I am grateful to have worked at the place that enhances each client's journey, makes it easier, and helps clients keep a destination in sight.

BETSEY WALTERS

Baskets

I have been involved with Minneapolis Society for the Blind, which we now know as Vision Loss Resources, for many years. I received adjustment-to-blindness training, and through the years, I have received a lot of support and information that has greatly enriched my life. When Vision Loss Resources started the Community Center, I found that I had new opportunities to interact socially, to learn new crafts, and to have a lot of fun. I looked forward to the Community Center calendars. One day, I received the calendar with a listing that made me jump for joy. "Basket Weaving! Wow!"

I fell in love with baskets when I was a child, and I had always wanted to learn to make them. I do not know why baskets had such an attraction for me. Perhaps it was because they were made from natural materials. Maybe it was because they were beautiful as well as serviceable.

I was surprised when I got to my first class; I had no idea that I would meet such delightful people. Our teacher, Frank Alden, was kind and endlessly patient with each of us. The dear volunteer who was there to assist Frank was just as kind and patient. It truly amazed me that I could take a bunch of sticks and turn them into a beautiful, useful basket.

And Frank—what can I say about him? I have never known anyone who has so much knowledge and who was such a good teacher. He remained cheerful and gracious, no matter what disaster cropped up in the sometimes not-so-smooth course of weaving baskets. Frank was great at smoothing out life's difficulties, offering advice, observations, his own experience, and just plain good humor and perspective. We would often talk about things that were going on in our lives that might not have been easy to cope with, to give each other support. Sometimes, one of us would wonder how to do something, like label a product or prepare a dish or some other barrier we would like to overcome. We would all chime in with ideas and solutions. Frank would broaden our horizons by introducing a new basket pattern, a new recipe, a new approach to an old issue, a new book to read, and many other ideas.

Frank's various assistants and coworkers were a treat. Stacy Shamblott was a good advocate for us, good-humored and fun with a strong sense of right and wrong. If she felt something was wrong, she put all her energy into making it right. Even when Stacy was having her own challenges, she was unfailingly cheerful. If she was struggling with crutches or some other health issue, she never moped or complained.

Jean Johnson was a great assistant in the basket-weaving classes, too. She shared so much with us, from great recipes and cooking techniques to new advances in technology. She worked on her own baskets so she could have a sense of how we were constructing ours.

We had so much fun exchanging ideas about color and textures and approaches to the weaving process.

The baskets themselves were special. I frequently use them for gifts. I filled some with baby clothes and toys for a baby-shower gift. I filled others with my hand-knitted dishcloths and handmade soap, which I learned to make at another Vision Loss Resources class, for bridal-shower gifts. I filled baskets with cookies and candy and other edible treats for birthday and thank-you gifts. One of my friends who is involved with a dog rescue group asked me if I would donate some of my baskets to their fund-raising drive. I gave her some of my small baskets, and she filled them with dog treats and sold them. I had a friend who opened his own business. With help from Frank, I wove a set of baskets for his new office—a business-card basket and in-and-out baskets. I use a basket for my gardening equipment, and I have a mail basket I made where I keep my mail sorted.

One of the best aspects of the classes was the other students. We had such a great time, exchanging stories and ideas. Basket-weaving classes were more than just the chance to make a pretty basket that could either end up being a nice present for just about any occasion or something beautiful that made you feel good about your own accomplishments. We had the chance to meet each other, share with each other, and support each other. For ten years I attended those basket-weaving classes. I met lovely, interesting, funny, very dear people that I count among my lifelong friends. We were blessed with knowing Frank. Those classes were some of the best times of my life.

LORI McCLURE
Vital Life Restored

E veryone faces challenges. I faced a major one at the age of seven when I was diagnosed with a degenerative eye disease, retinitis pigmentosa, commonly called RP. Slowly and cruelly, it stole my vision. Fast-forward to my forties: my vision had deteriorated to light perception only. My life as I knew it was over. I thought I was too old to learn anything new. But my faith in God helped me realize I was too young not to try.

State Services for the Blind provided me the opportunity to be a full-time student at the Rehabilitation Center at Vision Loss Resources, also known as VLR. The Adjustment to Blindness program offered the following courses: braille, woodworking, keyboard, computer technology, leisure ed, food prep, techniques of daily living, and orientation and mobility (cane training).

I was reluctant to take woodworking classes, as I wasn't exactly a handywoman and had never worked with power tools. My instructor showed me a finished birdhouse and said, "How about just giving this a try, and if you don't like it you can quit." I thought that was fair, so I agreed. The instructor always showed me the safe and proper way to use the tools and equipment.

I used a drill press to make the hole in the birdhouse and a saw to cut a piece of wood for the perch. After accomplishing this, I was hooked! The buzzing and hissing of the tools was very intimidating, however. I wondered if I would slip up and have a bad accident if I continued with other projects. The instructor was always by my side and made sure my hands were in the proper position to operate the power tools. I was in this class for almost a year. It continually amazed me that I was having fun. I thought this was the one class I wouldn't like and would probably give up on. It's hard to explain, but over time, as my projects came together, the whole process just grew on me. The fear gave way to enjoyment. I went on to make an oak serving tray, a closet organizer, and a hope chest, all of which I'd designed. I used a table saw, miter saw, and electric sander. Who knew power tools would be so much fun!

I also decided to try the braille class. I told my braille instructor when I put my hand on a page of braille dots I thought I'd never learn to read that mess. She said, "You only have to learn to read it a letter at a time." That's exactly what I did, and it wasn't as difficult as I'd imagined. Are you familiar with dice? If you look at the dots forming two vertical lines on the number six, you know what a braille cell looks like. All the numbers and letters of the alphabet are formed utilizing different combinations of these dots. The dot in the upper left is dot one. The middle dot is dot two and the bottom left is dot three. The upper right is four, followed by five in the middle and dot six in the bottom right. The letter A is dot one. The letter B is dots one and two. C is one and four. The word cab, for example, is dots one and four in the first cell, followed by dot one in the second cell, and dots one and two in the third cell. When you memorize the alphabet and recognize the pattern, it gets easier with practice. This is called grade one braille. In grade two, you learn contractions, other combinations that will use single letters for entire words, and punctuation. I have always had an excellent memory, which helped me immensely. Consequently, I became quite proficient in reading and writing braille.

In addition to feeling apprehension about learning woodworking and braille, I felt overwhelmed at the thought of learning keyboard and computer because I hadn't taken typing in high school. I learned to type despite the fact I'd never seen the letters on the keyboard. I wore headphones and listened to a tutorial on typing while JAWS, the screen-reading software, announced each key as I typed. I disliked learning this way, but I enjoyed it once I got the hang of it. I'm still in the process of learning computers. There are days when I get frustrated and want to throw my computer out the window!

In the leisure ed class, I learned about games adapted for the visually impaired. For example, you can get a Scrabble game with grids on the board so that when you touch the tiles, which are brailled with the letters and point values, they won't slide around. Moreover, you can buy or make your own playing cards with the suits and numbers marked in braille. Cribbage boards can be made with grommets around the pegging holes so you can keep score much easier than with a regular board. The instructors taught me how to make several handmade crafts, too. The leisure time was a nice break between the mind-boggling braille and tech classes. The variety of things I worked on taught me how to organize, work independently, problem solve, and think creatively.

One of my favorite courses was food prep, which wasn't necessarily a cooking class. The main objective was learning how to use knives, gadgets, and other equipment safely in the kitchen. We were also taught many helpful hints for performing tasks without vision. Some of these hints included measuring wet and dry ingredients, pouring liquids, and determining when food was cooked or baked the proper amount of time. Since I'd been a homemaker for over twenty years, I didn't have a problem using knives or other tools without sight. But, the thought of using the gas stove in my new home made me nervous. All my life I'd cooked on electric ranges. My instructor was very patient and helped me get over my fear of the gas burners. Long oven mitts, proper placement of pan handles, and the right tool for the task you were performing were important safety lessons. After many months and numerous classes without mishap, she helped me realize I could work safely with gas. I brought home many great dishes from these Monday afternoon classes. As I practiced at home, I regained enough confidence to start cooking again.

In the techniques of daily living class, I learned how to do household chores, identify money, use signature cards, and much more. Learning these things was invaluable!

Orientation and mobility was the toughest course of all. First I had to learn how to hold the cane properly and walk in step correctly. Learning to do this was necessary before I could walk down a hallway or sidewalk, let alone cross a street. The prospect of crossing by myself without sight terrified me. I knew other blind people did it all the time, but I thought I'd never go anywhere by myself so it wasn't necessary for me to learn. Despite my fears, I knew somewhere deep inside me everything my instructor was trying to teach me was for my own good. I soon learned that to cross safely you have to determine whether or not the intersection is controlled with stop signs or traffic lights. You have to listen for vehicles turning and then listen for the surge of traffic. When I didn't have the edge of a lawn, building, or curb to line up with, I tended to veer to the right in crosswalks. This often led to my walking into the traffic lane or into the front of a vehicle, which was scary and dangerous.

One day, my instructor helped me just cross

intersections over and over until I improved enough to cross safely on my own. I stood at the corner and tried to concentrate on each skill I'd been taught. After crossing the four corners of a busy intersection several times, I stepped up on the curb and was greeted by applause. A man's voice said to me, "Good for you. We've been watching, and you're getting better." He explained that he and his buddy were curious and had stopped to observe. I told them what I was doing, and they wished me good luck and hoped I would stay safe. At first I was embarrassed by their scrutiny. Later, it made me feel good to know there were kind folks who cared.

Another part of the mobility course entailed learning to use the public bus system, locating and identifying specific prearranged addresses, and finding my way inside buildings to determine if I was at the right location. One day I was walking in downtown Minneapolis, near Orchestra Hall, and had to walk several blocks to my bus stop on Hennepin Avenue. I wasn't very familiar with this area and felt frightened and alone. There was road construction nearby, and the sound of jackhammers covered up the sounds of pedestrians and traffic. I was on the verge of tears and wanted to throw my hands in the air and quit. I started to pray and called out to God, asking for his help. All of a sudden I felt a bright light, like a sunbeam, appear in front of my feet and make a path for me all the way to my bus stop. I remember thinking

I was like Dorothy following the yellow brick road. As I arrived at my bus stop, I had a huge smile on my face. I knew from that moment forward all my steps would be safe.

Upon the completion of orientation and mobility lessons, Vision Loss Resources clients receive, as a reward, breakfast or lunch at a restaurant of their choosing. We must meet the prerequisite, though, of taking at least one bus ride on our own. I chose Keys Cafe in downtown Minneapolis. This independent trip took two bus rides and was worth every step. My instructor met me there, and we had a terrific breakfast. This trip, taken on May 26, 2004, made my fiftieth birthday a day I'll never forget!

When I finished taking all the classes and was about to graduate, I realized I had a sense of independence and self-confidence I hadn't had before. Living with blindness wouldn't be the bad, sad, scary, or lonely existence I thought it would be. While thanking my instructors at my graduation ceremony, it occurred to me that from now on VLR would not only stand for Vision Loss Resources, but also for vital life restored.

Contributor Biographies

"**A MOM**" believes her daughter is an exceptional teacher and guide. Mom is forever proud of her daughter's guidance and accomplishments. Her daughter teaches her something new every day that enhances life, shapes the definition of dignity, and raises the bars of value and integrity. Over the past thirty years, Mom has experienced things that she never imagined she'd experience while being a parent.

CAROL ALPERIN is a wife, a mother of three, a proud grandmother, and an animal lover. An experienced knitter/crocheter/crafter, Carol thoroughly enjoys interacting with and teaching other blind individuals creative techniques to enable them to learn new skills or continue activities they enjoy. She likes writing, reading, music, houseplants, and more recently, peer counseling; she's rewarded by the challenge of motivating others.

ROBERT ANDERSON believes his blindness forced him inward to discover hidden gifts of creativity, spirituality, empathy, and service. His ex-wife once said he was a better person when he was hurting. Blindness hurt real bad. His poems and essays have appeared in numerous publications, and he's won awards and fellowships from The Loft and other state arts organizations. He's published a memoir, *Out of Denial,* and is currently writing a sequel exploring the spiritual coming-out process. He lives in St. Louis Park with his partner, John.

SUSAN ANDERSON has worked in the human services field for over ten years. Choosing a vocation that involves working toward the betterment of others has always been important to her. One of the lessons she was taught as a child was that we should leave things better than the way we found them. That lesson has been the underlying theme in her passion to help others, beautifying a space with art, and raising her two little bug-a-boos.

HELEN BARTLETT is proof that you can't tell a book by its cover. By using adaptive technology, she can adapt to vision loss and write poetry, essays, and children's books. In addition, she is a member of several book groups.

C. L. BODER lives in Fridley with her husband Dan, two cats, and six birds. She attended the school for the blind in Faribault until her senior year of high school. After two years of college as a journalism major, she quit to get married. She has two children and four grandchildren. Writing is her avocation.

GARY BOETTCHER works at Opportunity Partners. He and his guide dog, Italy, enjoy going to elementary schools to give educational talks about blindness and working-dog issues. He enjoys spending time with his girlfriend, playing cards with blind friends, going out to restaurants with friends through Vision Loss Resources, watching sports, and playing Fantasy Football. He writes, "God has given me the blessing of my church and the friends. They continue to support me with love and encouragement, which makes my life as a blind person much easier."

VANESSA BONN writes, "I was diagnosed with retinitis pigmentosa: Bardet-Biedl when I was thirteen years old. My family is always amazed to see how I can scrapbook on my own and hike and camp with my husband, Randy. Having no peripheral vision and only some useable vision isn't always easy. My teaching degree in elementary education has brought me to work in the classroom and to my current career as a Tutor Connect coordinator. My faith in God, my supportive family and husband, and my 'go with the flow' attitude has helped me through my journey with vision loss."

JEAN CHRISTY is a longtime assistive technology instructor in the Rehabilitation Center at Vision Loss Resources. When asked how long she has worked at Vision Loss Resources, Jean often responds, "I used to have long dark hair, now I have short gray hair." Jean's studies in the areas of special education and psychology have been helpful in teaching adults who have recently lost vision. Jean's personal use of speech and large print devices reinforces their importance in people's lives.

JOHN LEE CLARK wishes there were one hundred hours in a day so that he could spend ninety-two of them writing and the remaining eight getting his beauty sleep. Nevertheless, his work has appeared in many publications, including *The Chronicle of Higher Education*, *McSweeney's*, *Poetry*, and *Sign Language Studies*. His chapbook of poems is entitled *Suddenly Slow*, and his first full-length collection is forthcoming. He also edited the anthologies *Deaf American Poetry* and *Deaf Lit Extravaganza*. He lives with his wife and their three sons south of Minneapolis, enjoys tandem cycling (longest cycling trip thus far: San Francisco to Los Angeles along the Pacific coast, 450 miles), and sometimes startles women in yarn stores when he buys supplies for his knitting projects.

JESS CRELLY grew up in the Twin Cities. When she was little, she wanted to be a chef and make tasty treats for other people to enjoy. Jess started college in southwestern Minnesota, taking culinary classes. By the end of the first year, she knew she did not want to work in a kitchen; she wanted to work with people. Jess switched schools and ended up at the University of Wisconsin–La Crosse, where she graduated a couple of years later with a degree in therapeutic recreation. Before coming to work at Vision Loss Resources, Jess worked in long-term care, planning and leading activities in a memory care unit. She enjoys working with people and improving their quality of life.

KATHY D'AVIA worked for twenty-four years in the main office of General Mills in Minneapolis. She writes, "Vision Loss Resources is the best thing that happened to me after I lost my vision. It gave me a can-do attitude on life. It taught me mobility, cooking, and crafts, as well as how to be independent. I volunteered for some time as a peer counselor and also taught JAWS, the screen-reading program."

JENNIFER DUBBIN was born in Little Falls, Minnesota, and is a graduate of Southwest Minnesota State University.

She is employed as the office manager for Employment Endeavors, an agency that helps people who are deaf or blind seek employment. Her guide dog, Liberty, is a golden Lab cross. She enjoys scrapbooking, soap making, knitting, watching TV and spending time with friends.

PAMELA R. FLETCHER serves as a writer, editor, and educator—all three roles, having words at their core, collaborate to make meaning of an astounding, outrageous world. She's tried to leave words, but they wouldn't give her a divorce. Although it's a contrary relationship, they make it work.

DELORES FORD likes to walk, quilt, and keep busy.

MARION FRIEDMAN was born in Minneapolis in 1921, graduated from high school in Grand Forks, North Dakota, and moved back to Minneapolis when she got married. She was a Vision Loss Resources support group facilitator for five years and a peer counselor for eight. She also was active in Vision Loss Resources' advocacy group.

NANCY FRITZAM is from Lewiston, Minnesota. She has been visually impaired since birth. She attended the Minnesota School for the Blind and got a degree in social work from the University of Minnesota. In 2009, she retired from the Social Security Teleservice Center after working there for twenty-seven years. Now she has lots of time for family, hobbies, and friends.

KATI GALLAGHER grew up in Minneapolis, moved to Florida in 1984, and came back home to Minnesota in 1999.

Her work history is varied: ASL interpreter, ASL instructor, admissions counselor, massage therapist, bookseller, and assistant director for a nonprofit.

KATE GRATHWOL, PhD, is the president and CEO of Vision Loss Resources. Before working in vision rehabilitation services, Kate was a nationally exhibited photographer. She is an avid sailor and hiker, and can sometimes be seen skipping around south Minneapolis, where she lives with her husband, Barry, and their dog, Java.

BEVERLY HAALAND-SAVAGE traded in her dancing shoes and dedicated time to family and a master of arts degree in educational psychology at the University of Minnesota. At present, Bev is enjoying newly acquired computer skills, especially reconnecting with extended family and friends from childhood via Facebook and email.

GARY HENTGES is a woodworking instructor at Vision Loss Resources and has a setup in his garage where he does hobby woodworking. He also enjoys the Minnesota Twins, working out on his stationary bike at home, going for long walks, and watching old movies, particularly John Wayne movies. He's also very interested in other people and what they are doing, and enjoys talking to others at Vision Loss Resources.

WALLY HINZ arrived in this world April 15, 1942, a hell of a tax deduction for Chuck and Addie Hinz. He has been involved in athletics in grade school, high school, college, and beyond. He currently is a member of the board of directors at Vision Loss Resources and a lifelong athletic supporter. Wally is a great storyteller and is thrilled at this opportunity to write down some of his stories to be shared with others.

As an occupational therapist, **TARA ARLENE INNMON** began losing vision. She then started painting, exhibiting across the United States. She asked the universe what she should do when she won't be able to paint anymore. She saw a bolt of lightning and heard a voice in her head bellow, "You will write!" After she became totally blind, she graduated with an MFA in creative writing at Hamline University. She is writing a memoir.

LYN JOHNSON was born and raised in St. Paul and currently resides in Oakdale. She has been legally blind for about five years. Instead of searching for that painter, she probably should be looking for the lawmakers who established the guidelines—assuming such guidelines do exist—for that painter to follow.

KELLY likes to use the languages of French, Swedish, and Finnish; to play piano if people enjoy singing; and to rename files on her PAC Mate. She has been blind since birth. She adores braille and says she will keep braille forever, until the end of time. "Braille will always stick to me like glue."

JERRY KLOSS is a lifelong resident of the Twin Cities who was employed at MnDOT for thirty-five years and at the Courage Center for ten years. He is interested in ham radio and is a member of Handiham. He enjoys singing in the Plymouth Rockers, a sixty-five-person senior group that performs about forty concerts yearly at various senior care facilities. He's proud to serve Vision Loss Resources in any way he can, as the agency has come to his aid in the past, and continues to do so.

DAWN KULTALA is an aunt, a painter, and the mom of a seventeen-year-old.

LINDA LEANGER is a twenty-year volunteer peer counselor for Vision Loss Resources. She enjoys interacting with others and helping them adjust to vision loss. She's a wife, mother, and proud grandmother, and she is crazy about a cocker spaniel named Charlie. Known as the "pink lady," she's not totally happy unless she's wearing some shade of pink. She likes reading, writing, doing crafts, playing games, baking, and socializing.

NIKI MATTSON is currently a volunteer at United Hospital, in the Patient Discharge Services department, assisting in transporting her patients to the front lobby to go home, delivering flowers to patients' rooms, and bringing medications to rooms and the different pharmacies in the hospital. She loves animals, particularly cats, and has studied online at Penn Foster Schools, where she received her degree as a veterinary assistant. She also has volunteered in a feline-only shelter, socializing cats to be adopted while cleaning their cages. She also likes to play beep baseball and is on a recreational team with some friends.

Faith, family, and friends are most important to **LORI MCCLURE**. She is an avid reader and a sports fan, and loves trivia and board games. Since losing her sight, she has served on an advocacy committee and as a support group facilitator. She's also served on the board of directors of Vision Loss Resources for six years. Currently, she is a peer counselor, working with visually impaired clients.

CYNTHIA MCFADDEN has a BA in English and a master's in library science. She worked at South Dakota State University for twelve years and was library director in Ogallala, Nebraska, for three years. She spent more than six years at Arapahoe Library District in Colorado. Cindy enjoys cooking and baking. Currently, she's taking ballroom dance lessons, which is on her bucket list.

LOUIE MCGEE is currently a seventh grader at Highland Catholic School in St. Paul, where he lives with his mom (Annie), dad (Greg), and younger sister (Carmella). He is very active in sports (soccer, track, swimming, and skiing), and works hard to raise money and awareness for blindness-related causes. Louie has been speaking and writing about blindness for the past three years, and hopes to continue to share his experiences and motivate kids to find a cause they can get passionate about.

JEFF MIHELICH is a participant on several boards that advocate for the blind/low-vision communities. He and his partner live in south Minneapolis, in a cute little double bungalow with a wonderful retreat in the back yard. "It is always a challenge to stay one step ahead of the rabbits and squirrels. Replacing plantings they think are just perfect for dinner."

ELLEN MORROW has been a counselor at Vision Loss Resources since 1977. She came to the organization as a young mom and is now a grandmother of six! She is privileged to serve the people of Vision Loss Resources, whom she considers the best part of working for the organization.

MARY NICKLAWSKE has a BA in sociology from the College of Saint Benedict and a master's degree in orientation and mobility from Western Michigan University. Mary has taught clients to travel confidently and independently for the past twenty-four years in Chicago, Connecticut, Minnesota, and Ireland. She feels incredibly lucky to have had the opportunity to work and learn with people of all ages and walks of life. Mary has enjoyed all the great adventures her clients have taken her on in their quest to gain independence. In her spare time, Mary enjoys hanging out with her son, Leo, and her husband, Barry. She loves the outdoors and enjoys running, hiking, biking, cross-country skiing, and traveling. Mary's favorite quote is from Helen Keller: "Life is either a daring adventure or nothing." She currently lives in White Bear Lake, Minnesota.

DIANE O'SHAUGHNESSY has been a volunteer for Vision Loss Resources for several years. She has lost most of her vision to a retinal disease, so she has given up her inevitable misadventures in horseback riding and skiing for a more innocuous, yet exhilarating, lifestyle of dancing, audio reading, and writing. Her magic moment was seeing this book evolve from fantasy to fruition.

SUE OLSON graduated from nursing school in 1982 with an LPN degree. She is a published poet and loves to make people laugh. She retired from Medtronic in 2003, where she taught computer classes as well as chemical and fire safety. She also kept records for the FDA. Sue has been married for seven years to Chris and has a twenty-year-old daughter. She enjoys volunteering, making crafts, and cooking.

SUZANNE PAULUK has a BA in English, with a Spanish minor. She has belonged to the Christian Writers Guild and writes and edits the Care & Share Ministry newsletter for the ministry she and her husband have for people with disabilities. She loves working for WeCo, testing websites and electronic documents for accessibility using a magnification and screen-reading program.

MAUREEN PRANGHOFER is busier than an ant in a sugar bowl. She has worked in the fields of music therapy, social work, and advocacy, and currently runs an in-home business transcribing materials into braille. She is a songwriter with three CDs containing original music and lyrics. In her spare time she enjoys reading, knitting, and doing things with her husband of thirty-five years.

JOHN PRIESTLEY worked at MoneyGram for the past eighteen-plus years and now is semiretired. He has been married to Jennifer for over forty years. He likes to tease her when the power goes out and lights go off by saying, "Well, now we're on a level playing field!" He is on his fourth guide dog, all with different personalities! He likes to ride a tandem and has ridden in some MS 150s.

ERIN E. C. SALINAS, a registered occupational therapist, is a native Minnesotan who spent seven years living in Oaxaca, Mexico. She lives in Columbia Heights with her husband, two rescued dogs, and a parrot, who shows no interest in learning to say "I love you," but whose vocabulary includes the phrase "Why must I be surrounded by idiots?"

Except for dull term papers, this, truly, is **JULIETTE SILVERS**'s first writing attempt. She enjoyed it more than she expected. New technology makes the process much easier than in the past. Juliette currently leads support groups at Vision Loss Resources and volunteers with the Minnesota Literacy Council teaching adults English as their second language. Of course, they have to put up with her New York accent. Juliette lives with her two adoring cats in south Minneapolis.

CORALMAE "COKE" STENSTROM was born and educated as a nurse in Michigan, lived in Illinois for forty-six years, and was widowed after forty years. She has three children and three grandchildren. Coke has sung in five choirs, sewed and donated hundreds of children's sundresses, and donated gallons of blood. Her longest job was twenty-eight years as a psychiatric nurse. Coke loves gardening, hats, knitting, traveling, and friendships. She moved to Minnesota in 2000.

AMY SUMMER has been a client with Vision Loss Resources since 2005, when a change in her vision brought her back to the organization. Her first contact with Vision Loss Resources, however, was as a volunteer in high school, when the organization was then known as Minneapolis Society for the Blind. She lives in Minneapolis and works in the environmental field. So far, she hasn't found a piece of plastic she can't reuse, reduce, or recycle.

KAY TRAPP writes, "I have always loved to write. I was a teacher for many years. I love working with children and am now tutoring children from three countries. I spent ten years in Australia, and since the kangaroos didn't need to learn how to hop, I taught children in the outback. It was great teaching kids who loved school because they didn't have anything else vying for their time. Therefore Australia is my favorite subject to write about. I can't teach in a regular classroom because of my vision, but I can still work with children, and I appreciate Vision Loss Resources for opening the door to writing and allowing me to write and keep alive my memories of teaching in Australia."

VINCE ULSTAD grew up on a farm in west-central Minnesota. He attended Moorhead State University and North Dakota State University, graduating with a plant sciences degree. He has served in a number of capacities in the agricultural industry, primarily in product and market development functions in the north-central and western regions of the United States and western Canada. His life-long interests and hobbies include camping, hiking, backpacking, canoeing, boating, fishing, ballroom dancing, bicycling, landscaping and gardening, farming, pheasant hunting, woodworking, and reading.

DIANA BEUCLER VANASSE is a former teacher of middle-school autistic students. She began losing her vision about eleven years ago, and she has undergone many life changes due to this loss. Currently, she is involved with many activities at Vision Loss Resources in both Minneapolis and St. Paul. Diana has two married sons and six grandchildren who have experienced this loss with her.

DENA WAINWRIGHT is originally from Canada. She has a master's degree in rehabilitation psychology from the University of Wisconsin, and teaches technology at Vision Loss Resources. She attends the Adler Graduate School with the hope of counseling people with disabilities and their families. Her passions include music, writing, and being a mom to her young daughter.

BETSEY WALTERS has woven a full life for herself through education, training, and work. She credits basket weaving with adding a new, joyful dimension to that busy life.

LINDA WALTZ is the sole proprietor of A Helping Touch for Wellness. She is a wellness coach, light worker, and certified therapeutic bodyworker. Her greatest passion is uncovering clues, unraveling mysteries, and drawing open the curtain on the magical power of love. Her favorite ways to pass the time include loving her animal companions, spending time in nature, holding babies, dancing, knitting, basket making, quilting, and beading.

FRANCES WHETSTONE and her husband moved to Minneapolis fifty-six years ago. Frances knew no one, but believes "you have to get out and meet people." Now ninety-six years old, she has a wide circle of friends and serves on the Rehabilitation Council for the Blind, Senior Services committee, and is a peer counselor. She sends a shout-out to Vision Loss Resources President Kate Grathwol for her outstanding help.

PEGGY R. WOLFE, a feisty eighty-three-year-old with macular degeneration, authored *Macular Disease: Practical Strategies for Living with Vision Loss* (2011) and *Vision Loss: Strategies for Living with Hope and Independence* (2014). When her ballet class held a surprise party on her eightieth birthday, with piles of strawberries as the "cake," Peggy flitted across the floor, shouting her new slogan, "Eighty Power! Eighty Power!"

DEBBIE WYGAL has been a biology professor at Saint Catherine University for more than thirty years. She teaches a variety of courses; genetics is her favorite. When she is not preparing lectures and grading papers, she loves reading novels, being in two book groups, swimming, kayaking, riding her recumbent tricycle, and being with dogs, especially her springer spaniel, Bailey.

ELAINE ZUZEK has deep roots in Hastings, Minnesota, where she grew up. She was an RN for more than thirty-five years and now volunteers in the community. She is a member of a Hastings Lions Club and Vision Loss Resources' support group. She has seven married children and sixteen grandchildren, who all live nearby. She prescribes involvement and humor for dealing with loss.